Seeds For The Season

Dr. Lee Ann B. Marino, Ph.D., D.Min., D.D.

91 Days Of Breakthrough

SEEDS FOR *the Season*
91 DAYS OF BREAKTHROUGH
DR. LEE ANN B. MARINO, PH.D., D.MIN., D.D.

Published by:
Righteous Pen Publications
(*The righteousness of God shall guide my pen*)
www.righteouspenpublications.com

All rights reserved. Except as permitted under the U.S. Copyright Act of 1976, no part of this book may be reproduced, distributed, or transmitted in any form or by any means, electronic or mechanical, or saved in any information storage and retrieval system without written permission from the author.

Unless otherwise noted, Scripture quotations taken from the **Amplified® Bible, Classic Edition (AMPC)** Copyright © 1954, 1958, 1962, 1964, 1965, 1987 by The Lockman Foundation. Used by permission. (www.Lockman.org)

All Scripture quotations marked EXB are taken from **The Expanded Bible.** Copyright © 2011 by Thomas Nelson. Used by permission. All rights reserved.

All Scripture quotations marked KJV are taken from the **Holy Bible, Authorized King James Version,** Public Domain.

Book Classification:
Books > Religion & Spirituality > Worship & Devotion > Meditations

Cover and interior photos are in the Public Domain.

Copyright © 2018, 2025 by Lee Ann B. Marino

ISBN: 1-940197-47-3
13-Digit: 978-1-940197-47-0

Printed in the United States of America.

*Sometimes the things
we cannot change
end up changing us.
(Unknown)*

- Table of Contents -

	Introduction	1
1	Chronos vs. Karios	5
2	Rolling on the Floor, Laughing	9
3	None of Us are Where We Think We are	13
4	Fiona Grace	17
5	Just 'Cause I'm Quiet…Doesn't Mean I'm Over	21
6	Judging God	25
7	My Spiritual ABCs	29
8	When You are no Longer Doing it to Prove Something to Others	33
9	Some Journeys We Have to Make Alone	37
10	You Can't Crash Course or Fast-Track God	41
11	For Such a Time as This	45
12	Back to Basics – Very Basics	49
13	Just Upload the File Again!	53
14	You Can't Save Everybody	57
15	Typical is Typical	61
16	Embracing What You're Good At	65
17	Hiding Behind Tradition	69
18	Impatients	73
19	Empty Momentarily, Die Daily	77
20	Embracing My Inner (and Outer) Badness	81
21	…Why are You in My Life Again?	85
22	Same Type of Crazy as Me	89
23	Right Down the Street, Under My Nose	93
24	The Color of Favor	97
25	Just do it	101
26	Walking Around Naked	105
27	Distractions	109
28	I Can't do it With You – But I Can Still do it!	113
29	Becoming Foolproof	117
30	Is God Busy Watching Karachi?	121

#	Title	Page
31	The Man Upstairs	125
32	Surprises	129
33	Ain't Nobody got Time for That!	133
34	Small Wonders	137
35	Things Have got to Change	141
36	The Rosy Color of Hindsight	145
37	I'm not on Clearance!	149
38	When Others Interfere in Your Relationship with God	153
39	Still Hot as Hell	157
40	Becoming Neo-Apostolic	161
41	Coming to the End of Myself	165
42	Putting on the Shoes of Peace	169
43	A Little Bit Christian, a Little Bit Rock and Roll	173
44	Inspired Busyness	177
45	Fixing the Broken Nail	181
46	Divine Hints	185
47	Snap out of it!	189
48	White and Nerdy	193
49	Identification	197
50	Good Stewardship	201
51	I'm not Short, I'm Ultra-Concentrated Awesome	205
52	His Heart Trusts in Her	209
53	Ready to be Blessed!	213
54	Adventures in Vacuuming	217
55	Kicking and Screaming	221
56	A Sabbath Rest for the Minister of God	225
57	Happiness is...	229
58	Love and Eternity	233
59	Community	237
60	Be on Your Guard Against Men	241
61	Hearing God's Voice	245
62	Standing Through the Things That Have no Answer	249
63	Don't Let Me Get Me	253
64	Breaking the Habit	257
65	It Rains on the Just and Unjust Alike	261

66	What's Really Important?	265
67	Whatever	269
68	You Lie Like a Rug on the Floor	273
69	Pruning	277
70	Just Because I Don't Say Anything Doesn't Mean I Don't Know What's Going On	281
71	I Wish You Were Here	285
72	Our Father Who Art in Heaven	289
73	Hope Deferred	293
74	Gossip, Gossip, Gossip!	297
75	Meeting the Spirit Again for the Very First Time	301
76	My Name is no!	305
77	Learning About Faith Again and Again	309
78	Grace-Full	313
79	Going First	317
80	This is Who I Am	321
81	Measures of Faith	325
82	The Kingdom of God is Within You!	329
83	Rearranging	333
84	Our Sticky Situations	337
85	Needful Things	341
86	The Fullness of Time	345
87	Wide Awake	349
88	Selah	353
89	Crossing Borders	357
90	It Ain't Over Until the Heavenly Choir Sings	361
91	Divine Contradictions	365
	Afterword: The End of a Season	369
	About the Author	373

- INTRODUCTION -

WHEN I entered my last season in 2013, I had no idea what would befall me or anyone connected to me. At first, I didn't even realize I was in a new season. I just assumed things were the same and nothing was going to be very different.

Wow, was I in for a shock.

In this season, everything changed. I went from having a relatively conventional ministry with decent support to people leaving, throwing fits, creating all-out assaults, and some doors slammed shut by people I'd known a long time and trusted. Things went from a positive year in which I was going to minister in Europe for the first time to a disillusioned end of the year, where I feared getting sued by a church landlord. The year to follow wasn't much better, and it followed with its own complications. Continuing on and on, each year seemed to get worse and more complicated, up until I started getting the message about change. The people I was working with weren't the ones God wanted me to work with anymore. The more I watched people drop off and stop trying to replace them myself or pick some of them up, the more things started to become clearer. I was in a season. This was the way it was. Until everything that needed to be changed was to change, here was this season...with all its difficulties and understated glories.

In nature, a season's length is 91 days. Not all seasons are that short or that long in God of course, but they are compared to seasons because they are periods of time in which certain things related to the growing process occur. In nature, we can't have a proper growing season without the natural seasons of winter, spring, summer, and fall. We must have planting, growth, harvest, and rest. In our spiritual lives, we also go through seasons that relate in the same way. Sometimes we are planting, growing, harvesting, preparing the harvest, resting, pruning, and starting all over again. No matter how long or short a season may be, they always teach us something about others and ourselves, as well as our spiritual posture. If we pay attention to them, we can learn – and discover – amazing things.

There are two key words to note in the title of this book: the first word is "seeds", and the second word is "season." Each one of these daily devotionals reflects on lessons I have learned throughout this season. The lessons become "seeds" because at the end of each harvest, plants die and seed pods form for farmers or gardeners to retain for the next planting season. In my lessons, I have found seeds – experiences, stories, and thoughts to store and sow for the next season to some. In every season we prepare for our next one, and we should never get so caught up in where we are right now that we forget about later. The second word, "season," refers to both the length of this devotional, which is ninety-one days long, and the applied principle of whatever season you are in with God, no matter how long it takes. Whether your season is ninety—one days or nine years, you can apply the insights and thoughts found in this devotional, every day for as long as you need, to bring wisdom and insight to things you may be going through.

Lastly, the cover of our devotional features a dandelion plant after it has gone to seed. The original cover design was pretty and elegant, with purple flowers around it. This one was selected instead because it shows the dirt and grit that sometimes goes along with seasonal growth. Not everything about our spiritual lives is pretty. Growing in God means we go through some difficult, uncomfortable things and experience some hard, difficult places. I have selected the dandelion representation because as a weed, it finds a way to be drought and flood tolerant, to grow even though it's uprooted, and to shine in situations where people may ignore it or try to get rid of it. That is how we must root ourselves – and until we do, we will find our seasons most trying and unpleasant. Sometimes we need to get some resolve and model a weed, and make ourselves stay put, ready, willing, and able no matter the circumstances.

Whether where you are is dry and dusty or lush and fragrant, seasons have a way of coming around, changing, transforming, and ultimately, transforming us. No matter where you are right now, this book holds special promise to help you get through and prepare for the things that lie ahead for you next.

- Day 1 -
Chronos vs. Karios

NEVERTHELESS, DO NOT LET THIS ONE FACT ESCAPE YOU, BELOVED, THAT WITH THE LORD ONE DAY IS AS A THOUSAND YEARS AND A THOUSAND YEARS AS ONE DAY. THE LORD DOES NOT DELAY *AND* IS NOT TARDY *OR* SLOW ABOUT WHAT HE PROMISES, ACCORDING TO SOME PEOPLE'S CONCEPTION OF SLOWNESS, BUT HE IS LONG-SUFFERING (EXTRAORDINARILY PATIENT) TOWARD YOU, NOT DESIRING THAT ANY SHOULD PERISH, BUT THAT ALL SHOULD TURN TO REPENTANCE.
(2 PETER 3:8-9)

READING: ECCLESIASTES 3:1-11

I'VE never seen the hit musical *Rent*, but I discovered the music from the show right around the time that my difficult season began. I immediately clicked with the lyrics, especially those for the song "Seasons of Love." The song captures the essence of our concepts about time and about making our lives more than just time, more than just 525,600 minutes in a year, which was something I needed to hear. I was counting the number of years I had been in ministry and was feeling like something was lacking.

We've all heard it said, "God's time is not our time." It turns out this is very true. The way it's true is different from the way we often conceive, though, and the differences in our perception make it so we don't come to a place of understanding of God, or His timing, or the realities that make it so we can understand God better in our relationship with Him. We like to think of God on a timeline: operating when this, and this, and this happens, and if we do this, this, and this, then God will move. We try to capture God, put Him into our timing, and think if we work God well enough, we will outsmart God's divine system and get whatever it is we seek from Him.

The problem with this is, a) God is smarter than we are, and b) God's "time" isn't really time. We live in *chronos*, or chronological time, that moves like a timeline. We view our lives and days measured by past and future, seeing ourselves somewhere along that line. We tick off our lives as each 24-hour period goes by, wondering what might have been if we did something different or made different decisions. In seeing time through such a narrow view, we limit our concept of God and what He can do for us.

When we become believers, we are not just believing for right now or living for what we can see anymore. We are now living for things that we can't see and don't understand in our limited understanding of time. God is not within time; He is outside of time, not conditioned nor limited to our perceptions of time, nor required to comply with them. What we are required to do is conform to eternity, becoming a part of something that is bigger and greater than we can imagine in our infinite concepts of life and existence. In absorbing into eternity, which relates to *karios* time, we become better acquainted with prophetic time and understanding, learning to see things in a cyclical pattern rather than starting and ending permanently.

The ancients understood that things move in circles. The things we think we've achieved in *chronos* time, we probably have not achieved in *karios* time. We'll get a chance to prove whether we have attained the insight we seek spiritually, because the things that bother us, irk us, test us, and try us will come back, again, because the things that haunt us come back in their different forms, time and time again. If we accept karios, if we see how the spiritual works, then we will be better able to see that nothing goes away entirely, and no one goes away completely. Our goal is to rise above *chronos*, to rise above the limitations that we have placed upon us in this world and ascribe for a deeper understanding and meaning as we step forward and fully receive eternity.

- Day 2 -
Rolling on the Floor, Laughing

> HE SAID TO THEM, TO YOU IT HAS BEEN GIVEN TO [COME PROGRESSIVELY TO] KNOW (TO RECOGNIZE AND UNDERSTAND MORE STRONGLY AND CLEARLY) THE MYSTERIES *AND* SECRETS OF THE KINGDOM OF GOD, BUT FOR OTHERS THEY ARE IN PARABLES, SO THAT, [THOUGH] LOOKING, THEY MAY NOT SEE; AND HEARING, THEY MAY NOT COMPREHEND.
> (LUKE 8:10)

READING: 2 CORINTHIANS 8:8-16

WHEN I came into the season that inspired this book, I spent a lot of time in personal upset. Whenever someone left our ministry, it caused hurt feelings. Some of this was justified. Those who left often did so with disorder and upset (to others as well as to myself) and sought to do so in a hurtful way. It's hard not to take such things as a personal affront, especially when they are done toward you, to you, and as far as someone states, the whole point is that the issue is personal. That means I took it personal, as an attack on my leadership. It would send our organization into a spin with people picking sides. Words were exchanged, and chaos quickly ensued. It became about more than just who did what. It was also about the issue of leadership honor and ministry integrity. The problem with this is that it looked messy, at least from the outside looking in. We might have all had our reasons for feeling attacked and I certainly had reason for feeling that discipline was in order. The level that mess became, however, wasn't reasonable.

Over a period of about three years, for various reasons, we had several people leave the ministry. Most of the people who left were individuals who had been connected to the work for some length of time. We can't say they were fly-by-night. They were trusted individuals: an intercessor, an assistant, a pastor-in-training who was also a business partner, my best tither, one who claimed to be "ride-or-die," and one who came around and then go out from time-to-time but always seemed to make her way back. Some had to leave by disfellowship, some had their papers stripped, and some left of their own free will...but they all still left the ministry, most with hard feelings or actions and words that could not be taken back.

Then there was the aftermath.

At the time, the situations seemed larger than life. It felt like things would never find their balance again, and we couldn't easily move forward. Over time, things got back to normal. New people replaced the old. New problems came along that needed to be addressed. The thoughts and memories of those from times past began to fade into the background. One day, they didn't seem so important anymore. Things found their new normal, life became life again, and no matter what happened to those other people, we were still here.

It was still a surprise to see me burst out laughing, to the point where I fell out of my chair, when I learned one of these former seasonal individuals is now trying to start a mock "divinity school," charging participants $55.00 each to learn a system online that this individual borrowed and copied from some pastor out in California. You would have thought I would have been upset, and there would have been a time when I would have been. I would have wondered how he was doing it and why would anyone follow him, but nah...I just didn't care.

Progress comes in all forms. It doesn't always mean that you have more than everyone else or that you are doing something extraordinary that they are not. Sometimes it just means that you've learned to roll with the punches and take the absurd in good humor, because none of us can control what other people choose to do.

- DAY 3 -
None of Us are Where We Think We are

LISTEN TO ME, YOU STIFF-HEARTED *AND* YOU WHO HAVE LOST HEART,
YOU WHO ARE FAR FROM RIGHTEOUSNESS (FROM UPRIGHTNESS AND RIGHT STANDING WITH
GOD, AND FROM HIS RIGHTEOUS DELIVERANCE). I BRING NEAR MY RIGHTEOUSNESS
[IN THE DELIVERANCE OF ISRAEL], IT WILL NOT BE FAR OFF; AND MY SALVATION SHALL
NOT TARRY. AND I WILL PUT SALVATION IN ZION, FOR ISRAEL MY GLORY [YES, GIVE SALVATION
IN ZION AND MY GLORY TO ISRAEL].
(ISAIAH 46:12-13)

READING: EPHESIANS 4:21-32

POP culture church concepts about deliverance and being delivered have given us the impression that if we stop doing a certain thing, we are officially delivered from it. In a simplistic sort of way, I understand why this probably makes sense to some. It sounds good enough – if you stop or avoid whatever used to tempt you, it can't bother you anymore, right?

The truth is that we, as people, seriously overestimate ourselves and our abilities to avoid things on our own, as stemming from and extending out from our own will. We think we can do it all on our own and that avoiding our problem is sufficient enough to get us delivered. It isn't enough, and it doesn't work. If we don't set up points in our lives for accountability, reliability, and coming face-to-face with just who we are and what we battle, we will never see the deliverance we desire in our lives.

Throughout my season, I came face-to-face with several individuals who insisted they were delivered, healed, and set free...when it was obvious they were not. One such individual was a man who insisted he had been delivered from sex addiction. He might very well have not been out there sleeping with everything that moved, but he still had severe issues with power and control, dominance, and with women. Another woman had a long-term affair, to the point where she considered leaving her marriage. She always seemed to wind up back home or back with her long-term lover, alternating locations. She refused to cut ties with one or the other. Instead, she claimed to be friends with her adulterer. She claimed to be delivered, but instead of deliverance, it was obvious she found a way to get the best of both worlds and maintain those while keeping both men in a certain position in her life.

The demons they face, the spirits that pervade throughout their lives, and the things that they want most to be gone, remain right where they've always been. They manifest through power and control, a desire to be more spiritual than they are, and to prove something to everyone around them by outdoing them.

Competition in the Kingdom is a funny thing. It's something that shouldn't be there but often is. We have turned healing into a massive drive for acceptance, something to prove to others that we are just as Christian as they are and that we have just as much faith in God as the next person. We assume everyone else doesn't have the problems we do. In that drive to be perfect, we cover up, pretend, and force deliverance where it has never taken place.

All of us – every single person on earth, every single person in church – needs deliverance from something. It might not be the thing that gets the most talk from the pulpit and it most definitely might not be something we think about often enough, but the major thing every single one of us needs deliverance from is ourselves. We need to be delivered from the idea that we must be perfect, that we must be seen a certain way to be accepted, and that hiding our issues means we do not have them anymore. We will never be free until we are real with ourselves, and we will never be delivered if we insist we are free when clearly, we are not.

- Day 4 -
Fiona Grace

FOR IT IS BY FREE GRACE (GOD'S UNMERITED FAVOR) THAT YOU ARE SAVED
(DELIVERED FROM JUDGMENT *AND* MADE PARTAKERS OF CHRIST'S SALVATION)
THROUGH [YOUR] FAITH. AND THIS [SALVATION] IS NOT OF YOURSELVES [OF YOUR OWN
DOING, IT CAME NOT THROUGH YOUR OWN STRIVING], BUT IT IS THE GIFT OF GOD;
NOT BECAUSE OF WORKS [NOT THE FULFILLMENT OF THE LAW'S DEMANDS], LEST ANY MAN
SHOULD BOAST. [IT IS NOT THE RESULT OF WHAT ANYONE CAN POSSIBLY DO, SO NO ONE CAN
PRIDE HIMSELF IN IT OR TAKE GLORY TO HIMSELF.]
(EPHESIANS 2:8-9)

READING: GALATIANS 2:6-18

WHEN I first got my Labrador Retriever named Fiona, I couldn't decide if I wanted to name her Fiona or Grace. Fiona was my favorite character on the show *Burn Notice*, and the name "Fiona" means "white" or "bright" in Gaelic. Since Fiona has always been a dog with predominately white fur, the name seemed to suit her. Grace brought with it a sense of tranquility and peace, not to mention spiritual relevance. In the end, she became Fiona Grace, which suited her perfectly. Fiona from *Burn Notice* was a female mercenary, and had we put a gun in this dog's paws, she would have been Fiona. She was a difficult puppy who was rambunctious and often mean to my other dog, and she seemed to always be barking at someone. Fiona was a dog with something to say, who liked having her way, and who was ready at any time to go out for what she wanted.

To say that Fiona and I had issues is probably an understatement. I was used to having dogs I could sit and pet, but Fiona was too much of a fidget to ever do that. She didn't always do what she was told. She was sometimes difficult to love, but somewhere in here, I always loved her anyway. I named her "Grace" thinking she would be an instrument of grace in my life. Instead, she became a stark realization to me of what it meant to exercise grace.

Grace is one of those theological concepts that trips up theologians and scholars. I think it trips us up because in the natural world, we have a hard time understanding it. Some translate it as "unmerited favor," but in my own opinion, grace is more than just favor we don't deserve. It is a spiritual condition by which we are given something freely, without question, from the One Who doesn't have to give it to us. If we don't deserve it, then God doesn't have to give it, either. Grace is a statement of both what God does for us and what we are given and speaks truth about both the Giver and the receiver. As we take grace, it says something transforming about us, too.

Fiona Grace has been frustrating over the years, but during this particular season, I grew to see something in her that I wouldn't have readily otherwise embraced. As she ages, she's still her fiery, feisty self. She still barks at me when I tell her to come or to sit. She still wants to eat all the time. Difficult or not, she's an amazing dog with an amazing spirit who lets you know just where you stand with her. As hard as she is to love, I love her and tell her all the time what a sweet, pretty, good girl that she is. It might not be what she always deserves, but it's what she gets. She's mama's girl, and she reminds me every day of grace in my own life.

I call Fiona many things — FiFi, Fi, Fiona Grace Marino, Grace girl, Fiona Grace, and sometimes even Gracie — which roots and reminds me that she might not have been the reminder of grace I wanted to manifest, but she is certainly the memo of grace that I need. As God gives us grace, we don't deserve it, but He gives it because of Who He is. When I receive His grace in my life, it transforms me. When I display or extend His grace in my life, it's not because everyone around me deserves it, but because what He has done for me has transformed me.

If we want to better understand the reception of grace, we need to stand back and look at both the giver and the receiver and see where God's grace is speaking to us in this life. Here's to nine years and still going strong, my Fiona, my FiFi, my Fi, my Grace girl.

- DAY 5 -
Just 'Cause I'm Quiet...Doesn't Mean I'm Over

SO THE REALM OF JEHOSHAPHAT WAS QUIET, FOR HIS GOD GAVE HIM REST ROUND ABOUT.
(2 CHRONICLES 20:30)

READING: PROVERBS 1:22-33

THE first year of Sanctuary International Fellowship Tabernacle – SIFT was difficult, to say the least. I launched SIFT as Sanctuary Apostolic Fellowship and moved forward with the project after a great deal of prodding from God and others around me. It wasn't that I didn't feel the work was to come to fruition, but I wasn't sure as to how to do it. I'd started at least three other local church moves before that didn't go where I'd hoped they would. They all inspired other projects and moves that took off and flourished, but the local church concept never seemed to materialize for me in quite the way that it seemed to manifest itself for others. Our first year started off moderately strong, moving in what seemed to be a good direction. About halfway through, it was obvious that it wasn't going to turn out with the aspirations I had hoped. God brought His purposes to light, but that doesn't mean it was always easy. Accepting God's will for the situation as pertained to that first year was very difficult in ways that I couldn't imagine. There was part of me that felt like I was right back where I always was, all over again. People were angry, the staff I was supposed to be training got in a huff and left, and I was standing there, with a fraction of what we originally had, waiting to see what happened next.

As soon as the woman who was training to be pastor left

the church, she was very vocal. She announced she was doing a new company, no longer working with me, and attributed it to "personal growth." Within a few days, she launched a new website and was declaring herself to be things and have abilities she didn't have. I, on the other hand, got very quiet. Within weeks of her departure, we had to move out of our building due to a mold infestation. After sorting all that out and finding room for all our things, I had to refocus and see what was next.

In the process...I got quiet. Very quiet. Unusually quiet.

Others around me might have been making a lot of noise and generating a lot of attention for themselves, but I was quiet. I was thinking, processing, and waiting for my next moves. I needed to think about my anticipated future. To outsiders, some wondered where I went. I didn't splash all over the universe where I was or what I was doing next, because I just needed to be quiet. As a result, some thought I was done, over, finished.

I broke my silence with the message, "Just 'cause I'm quiet...doesn't mean I'm over" on social media. That was all I had to say. Just because I was quiet, doesn't mean everything as pertains to me was done. In reality, nothing was done. SIFT was still real; it was just transitioning. Ministry wasn't over because one person left; it was just being pruned a little. Life wasn't over because we had to leave the building; it just meant a new day was coming and a new place was necessary for change. Things weren't done, not by a long shot. I was simply processing and waiting out as the things that needed to change were changed.

We should be careful with what we assume to be over in both our own lives and the lives of others. Just because people get quiet, things are quiet for a little while, life changes, or things transition doesn't mean that something is over and done with all together. We all go through periods where we need quiet more than we need activity. this just means we need rest. Just as plants rest in the winter and come back to life in the spring, we too go through such periods in life. Quiet doesn't mean everything around us is finished forever.

- Day 6 -
Judging God

> Woe to him who strives with his Maker!—a worthless piece of broken pottery among other pieces equally worthless [and yet presuming to strive with his Maker]! Shall the clay say to him who fashions it, What do you think you are making? or, Your work has no handles?
> (Isaiah 45:9)

Reading: Luke 4:1-13

Have you ever judged God? I certainly have. I admit this so we can all be real and open about the realities of judgment. Truth be told, we've all judged God. We've all judged everyone and everything, and we haven't even been aware of it. We think that we're being inquisitive and interested when we judge God, just trying to be more in tune with Him. We tell ourselves all sorts of things, making it sound like nothing more than "inquiring minds want to know." What inquiring minds want to really do is judge.

Allow me to explain. Have you ever been in a situation and said "Why did God do this?" or "Why did God do that?" How about the infamous, "Why did God let this happen?" or the ever popular, "If God is good, why did God allow this?" If you haven't said it, I am sure you've thought it, or been around someone else who said it. The odds were good, whenever it came out of whoever's mouth, nobody had an answer for it. It was a statement that left people thinking about God and about the contradictory nature of the statement that if God is good, whatever was happening shouldn't have happened.

When we do this, we are judging God. We are

challenging His actions and claiming His nature is somehow not measuring up to being whatever our concept of God might be. We're stepping back and looking at God, making it clear that He is not being "God" enough or doing His job right, and we have it in our own minds that He should be doing something else...something more God-like, perhaps? Whatever happened doesn't feel like it should have, and we assume that God made a mistake somewhere in there. Maybe He got busy taking care of everyone else and took His eyes away for just one minute. Maybe He just didn't do something all the way or forgot.

Or maybe, just maybe, what needs to change is our concept of God.

When I started my spiritual season, I was one person, in one place, who had a specific concept of how God worked and what God should do. All throughout the season, I felt like God failed me in one way or another. When the money wasn't there, the people weren't following through, new people hadn't materialized, and I just didn't know what to do, I asked repeatedly why God was letting this happen. What I was really asking through the haze of frustration was why wasn't I getting my way about things. I was judging God because He wasn't doing for me what I wanted done, and I was missing the message in the process.

I don't think we realize how conceptual we are about God and how difficult it is to overcome those concepts, especially when we start getting the message that our concept of God is not exactly Who God is. In our most difficult times, God is revealing to us about His amazing nature and all that goes along with it. He isn't revealing it in so much of a theological way, but in a personal way that hits home for us, touching and reaching us so our understanding of Him can make a difference for us as people.

Yeah, we've all judged God. In that lesson, we all should learn how to let Him be God and see Him during our discomforts rather than in the confines of our comfortable doctrines and theologies that lead us nowhere.

- Day 7 -
My Spiritual ABCs

And we also [especially] thank God continually for this, that when you received the message of God [which you heard] from us, you welcomed it not as the word of [mere] men, but as it truly is, the Word of God, which is effectually at work in you who believe [exercising its superhuman power in those who adhere to and trust in and rely on it].
(1 Thessalonians 2:13)

Reading: Psalm 11:1-7

IN February of 2014, I was in a serious car accident. (It was obviously not fatal, and it was not as severe as many of the accidents I have seen people encounter.) It was serious enough to bang me up badly. My whole world changed the night a cab driver ran a red light and plowed straight into the side of the blue 2012 Ford Fusion in which I was a passenger. I spent the next two years dealing with chronic back pain that aggravated and subsided only to aggravate again, swelling in my body that left me looking disfigured, and difficulty with everyday tasks. I had to stop worship dance because I was in too much pain to move with the fluidity of the songs, and it rendered me unable to exercise or move without much pain. Most notably, it left me unable to sew. Given I have a design company, this was not good.

About four months after the accident, I got word from God to start a hand-sewn cross stitch project that would be displayed in our church sanctuary. I was excited because it was a kit I'd bought about a year earlier on a trip to New York to visit my mom. It consisted of 26 different blocks, one for each letter of the alphabet, with different spiritual things that started with each letter. "A" was Alpha and Omega, "B" was Bread of Life, "C" was Creator of all things, and so on and so forth. I could tell it was a showpiece right from the package, and I was ready to dive right in.

The problem with that was I couldn't sew like I could previously. Holding the fabric and the motion of the sewing aggravated all sorts of problems in my back, including sciatica, a pinched nerve, and upper back issues, which I never had before the car accident. I found I could only work on it for short periods of time. Even then, I had to go through long periods where I couldn't do it. It sat, I'd try to work on it, it would sit some more, and then it would take more time to do it. Given it was a 16"x20" design, it wasn't some small graphic that I could do overnight. It was a challenge.

It took me exactly two years and six months to complete a project that would have ordinarily taken me only a few months. By the time I got to the end of it, I never wanted to see it ever again. I was sick of outlines and lines. I was tired of the variegation I had to weave into the gold-colored border that consisted of three different shades. I was tired of the well-worn black-and-white pattern that was starting to fade in spots. I wasn't even sure if I wanted to do something else.

By the time I finished it, and I looked at it framed, I propped it up on the floor in admiration. Then, I noticed something in it that I hadn't considered. As I walked through my journey to heal, I had to go back over several spiritual "ABCs" myself. We all need that occasional reminder that inspires us to greater faith and encourages us to do better and bigger things, things that we never imagined possible at an earlier point in time. There's nothing wrong with foundations or reviewing the heartfelt concepts that we started and loved once upon a time. Sometimes we need to slow ourselves down, sit ourselves up, and try, try again to remember those basics and embrace them all over again. It might not be what screams progress to us, but there is a certain joy God takes in His children as they move from Alpha and Omega to King of Zion, hitting every topic in between, from beginning to end all over again.

- Day 8 -
When You are no Longer Doing it to Prove Something to Others

TAKE CARE NOT TO DO YOUR GOOD DEEDS PUBLICLY *OR* BEFORE MEN, IN ORDER TO BE SEEN BY THEM; OTHERWISE YOU WILL HAVE NO REWARD [RESERVED FOR AND AWAITING YOU] WITH *AND* FROM YOUR FATHER WHO IS IN HEAVEN.
(MATTHEW 6:1)

READING: JAMES 4:10-17

ONE of the dirty little secrets about ministry is the way ministers go out of their way to conform to the typical "preacher" image. Through years of ministering (especially in the realm of preaching), we learn quickly what to talk about and where to move what audience. If people are feeling good and enthusiastic, they'll think the Spirit is moving, whether it is or not. A lot of the time, preachers know what buttons to push, and they push them to get a likable rise out of their audiences. We know how to do it all: the right word to give at the right time, the topics to bring up seemingly out of nowhere that will charge and excite people, and how to pep up a slow audience with just the right blend of charisma and enthusiasm.

We also know how to interact with other ministers. There's a lot of truth to the fact that ministry protocols differ from ministry to ministry, but how to get invited back to the church is the same (at least most of the time). We know what to tell ministers to make them feel good about themselves and their work, what will move them to tears and inspire them to keep going, and what will make sure that we are their favorite preacher, time and time again.

I've never fit in well with preacher's circles because I've never been comfortable conforming to the expectations that exist. What we do is either about God or it's about us, or so that is the way that I see it. Trying to fit in with everyone else and what they are or are not doing doesn't suit me. If this isn't about God, then that means it's about us and trying to throng crowds to our pulpits. Either we got it, or we don't, and that's pretty much the beginning and the end of the whole matter.

I might not have agreed with it, but I was no stranger to toning down my messages or adjusting my preaching to wherever I might have been. I knew what topics to avoid, and I was good at avoiding them. I was the first one to admit that, on the surface, I was good at disguising my ministry as looking like all the rest, no matter how I felt about how things might have been done. So, when God called me to preach the message, "Guess Who's Coming To Dinner?" back in July of 2015, I knew that my support of the LGBTQ+ community would be noted, even though I spoke on it in an understated, yet not-so-subtle manner. I knew that those ministries who were on the fence about me to begin with were going to jump off that fence quickly. In the period it took to preach that singular message, I knew my entire life – and ministry – were going to change.

When I preached that message, my ministry officially stopped existing to please other people. As much as the word in church is to be different and we should stand out, I definitely got the message over years and years of ministry that my very existence should seek to model that which already exists without me. Forging our own way is discouraged through many stated and unstated principles, and through those concepts, we get the message that this ministry should be about others – not Christ.

That day, I stopped doing what I did for everyone else, and I found Christ in my own work again. It's a shame it ever got lost, but I know I am not the only one who has had to find their way back from the vast pathways of conformity.

- Day 9 -
Some Journeys We Have to Make Alone

THE LORD PROTECTS [GUARDS] THE FOREIGNERS [SOJOURNERS].
HE DEFENDS [SUPPORTS] THE ORPHANS AND WIDOWS [THE SOCIALLY VULNERABLE],
BUT HE BLOCKS [FRUSTRATES] THE WAY OF THE WICKED.
(PSALM 146:9, EXB)

READING: PSALM 91:1-13

WHEN my mom moved to North Carolina in 2015, we had no idea it would be over two years before she was able to find a house. There were days and weeks spent talking with one realtor, then another, then another, then a lender, and then another lender. The situation at hand was a little complicated for many reasons, and all those reasons boil down to one word: "unconventional." There was nothing conventional about my mom's situation. So, when the word came down about moving to Charlotte, the unconventional moving challenge got that much more unconventional. We'd come across several properties here and there, but nothing seemed to be just right.

Then there was the pretty, slate blue house that seemed like a decent option one January day in early 2017. Since I somewhat knew my way around Charlotte, we decided I would go look at the house and report back so a decision could be made. This sounds simple enough, but the instructions that went along with making the trip were, most decidedly, not. Whenever I make a stop in or through Charlotte, I almost always stop to visit people I know who live in that area. At the time of the trip, many of them were waiting to receive word that I was ready to move. My first inclination was to stop and visit with some who are there, to keep up morale and mutual edification. For this trip, however, that idea was out. God made it explicitly clear that I was to go to look at the house and then return home. I wasn't supposed to hang out, stay later, or visit with anyone.

I didn't protest, but I was curious what it was about this trip that made it so exclusive. In the first place, I wasn't the one buying the house. In the second, a little fellowship never hurt anyone. I am the biggest advocate that as Christians, we should get together with others and share as often as we can. So why the distance from others for the specific nature of this trip?

It turned out this trip to Charlotte was just one of those things I had to do on my own. It was one of those times where God calls us to stand on our own, away from others so that I could focus more on what He desired to tell me. Through the interaction with the realtor and through the thoughts of the trip, I needed the time and attention to focus on what I was doing, free from any thoughts or work I might encounter if I spent a lot of time with others. It wasn't that fellowship was bad; it was that I wasn't going to Charlotte to fellowship. This was one of those preparatory experiences where I had to go to get a word, to have an experience, and then to muse over it without the thoughts or opinions of others.

Sometimes we must do things on our own, without others. It's tempting to get so attached to others in our lives and to doing things with other people that we don't ever seek or desire to venture out ourselves. God works in community, God advocates accountability, and God does hold us responsible for the things that we do. He does require us to work and play well with others, as the expression goes. God also requires us to follow Him, and sometimes the places where we go, others can't easily come because they aren't supposed to go. Rather than hold on to the people of the past, God requires us come and walk, and make the journey with Him alone, instead.

- DAY 10 -
You Can't Crash Course or Fast-Track God

AND HE SAID TO THEM, BE CAREFUL WHAT YOU ARE HEARING.
THE MEASURE [OF THOUGHT AND STUDY] YOU GIVE [TO THE TRUTH YOU HEAR] WILL BE
THE MEASURE [OF VIRTUE AND KNOWLEDGE] THAT COMES BACK TO YOU—
AND MORE [BESIDES] WILL BE GIVEN TO YOU *WHO HEAR*.
(MARK 4:24)

READING: 2 TIMOTHY 2:15-19

OVER the course of my past season, I watched people I knew move at all different paces as pertains to their spiritual lives. Some were content with God, some were not-so-content, and others were ready to get on with whatever was next. In that season, I was all three. When I went into the season, I was very content with where I was. It might not have been where I wanted to remain throughout my life, but I was good with where I was. Then the discontent started, which lasted for the duration of the season. I was unhappy with the way things were, and I knew I needed a change. The problem was that I didn't know what it was that needed changing. I was content, mind you, with the state of the ministry. It was fine with me that on the surface we looked "typical" and was in no major hurry to fix that. So, when I started feeling incredibly discontented, I didn't know how to respond to it. As far as I was concerned, things were fine and didn't need to change. How I felt didn't go with what I was doing, and certainly didn't match what started to come along.

It didn't help that many of the people around me started experiencing their own discontentment. Many were quick to offer some advice, but they were so engrossed in their own things, they weren't often very much help. Later on, I would notice that as I started to figure things out, some got closer, some got further away, and others seemed to do something where they'd get far behind God and His work and then try to catch up at the last minute to where God is and whatever it was that He was doing. It reminded me of when we would be in school and refuse to study all semester long, only to get word of the mid-term or final and then cram the entire classwork's worth of reading and remembrance into one or two nights. We hoped that cramming last minute would give us the ability to complete our course, pass our test, and move past the terrible experience of severely being unprepared. The more I watched, the more I realized: we can't do this with God.

I came to this conclusion after looking at my own life and realizing how impossible it is to try and fast-track the process of God, especially when trying to figure things out. God's timing isn't easy to interpret. Figuring out whatever it is that God wants you to learn in a given period of time isn't easy to interpret. We only figure out what we need to learn in a given season as we walk it out and deal with our discomforts. There's no way to try and catch up on six months, a year, or two years' worth of learning and discipline with God in a weekend or a couple of weeks. This is why it's so often difficult to try and explain to other people what God is doing in your life. There's no way to summarize, catch people up, or explain it all in a few minutes. No matter how many questions someone might ask, it's not possible to fast-track God.

If you've missed out on what God is trying to do, then you've missed out on it and must start back at the beginning. We can't hope to miss out on the work of God for months or years and then expect to figure it all out by acting really devout or serious in only a short period of time. Yes, it can be tricky to figure out the movements of God, but we only find His true revelation to us if we are willing to stick through the difficult times and learn whatever He has appointed us to learn in this moment.

- DAY 11 -
For Such a Time as This

FOR IF YOU KEEP SILENT AT THIS TIME, RELIEF AND DELIVERANCE SHALL ARISE FOR THE JEWS FROM ELSEWHERE, BUT YOU AND YOUR FATHER'S HOUSE WILL PERISH. AND WHO KNOWS BUT THAT YOU HAVE COME TO THE KINGDOM FOR SUCH A TIME AS THIS *AND* FOR THIS VERY OCCASION?
(ESTHER 4:14)

READING: JOHN 4:21-26

I love the hit show *This Is Us* because it always gives me something to think about. For those who are unfamiliar with the show, *This Is Us* is about the lives of the Pearson family (complete with flashbacks). It shows the way their lives intersect and recalls things that happened earlier in time. The show revolves around twins Kevin and Kate (they were originally triplets, but one baby died) and Randall, a baby left at a fire station the day they were all born, who was then adopted by the Pearsons. In one episode, the entire hour is in flashback form: it recalls the day the triplets were born. It is Jack's birthday, and Rebecca, his very frustrated and pregnant wife, forgot his birthday. Once she remembered, she tried to make his birthday special. Later in the same episode, we saw the life of the doctor who delivers the triplets and encourages them to make the best of their situation as they face one of their triplets was stillborn (which also involves the death of the doctor's wife and the struggle to move forward without her), and the life of the fireman who finds Randall left at the station (who is trying to deal with a disconnected marriage).

What the show displayed was the way that many circumstances come together to meet with this little thing we like to call "timing." It wasn't just one thing that brought the situations and lives of these individuals together, it was all of it. It wasn't a matter of one person being ready or prepared, but of everyone moving in an abstract synchrony to bring the one cycle to completion and the next one to begin.

We like to talk about being here "for such a time as this," but I don't think we have the first clue of what it means. When we say that, we are usually talking about being in control of our destiny and moving into a place where we'll take on the whole world and change it. Yet *This Is Us* showed me that isn't really what it means. Just as Esther stood at the crux of many different situations and she had to think fast and act upon the many things that were happening all at once around her, so too we must meet a similar fate at different points in time. Esther was there because she could handle being a concubine, endless beauty treatments, going before the king, doing the right thing, and responding to the needs her uncle brought to her all the while with all the other circumstances going on around her.

When I came into my former season, I had no idea what being here "for such a time as this" meant. I used it like everyone else always does and never thought about it. Now having seen that show, I will never think the same way about it again. Being here for such a time as this isn't about trying to manifest or claim destiny for ourselves, it's about being able to recognize divine timing and see the way that different situations and circumstances come together. That's the advantage we have as believers: we can see the spiritual and discern the spiritual in every situation. We might not come away with the answer that we want (which is often to wait something out or give things more time), but we can, in each and every situation, step back and look for the timing to see if it is yet the "time such as this." If it's not, we keep pursuing until that time comes. It's hard to discern timing. I learned that throughout that season with God. What I learned is harder in such times is trying to make something "a time such as this" when it is not. Hold on and discern...and wait for things to come together in alignment.

- Day 12 -
Back to Basics – Very Basics

AND NOW I BESEECH THEE, LADY, NOT AS THOUGH I WROTE A NEW COMMANDMENT
UNTO THEE, BUT THAT WHICH WE HAD FROM THE BEGINNING, THAT WE LOVE
ONE ANOTHER. AND THIS IS LOVE, THAT WE WALK AFTER HIS COMMANDMENTS.
THIS IS THE COMMANDMENT, THAT, AS YE HAVE HEARD FROM THE BEGINNING,
YE SHOULD WALK IN IT.
(2 JOHN 1:5-6, KJV)

READING: HEBREWS 1:1-14

THE temptation to avoid humility always rises within us. What this means is that we like the idea we know things and we are confident in what we feel that we know. It seems like what we know outweighs what we don't know, and in the process, we start to puff up what we know far beyond reality.

I must admit, I never thought of pride in this form prior to my former season. I always thought that knowing was good, and knowing would lead to good things. Ideally, that's exactly what it should do, but unfortunately, it doesn't always work out that way. Sometimes the information we receive is wrong, which leads us into a place that deviates us far from where we are supposed to be. Sometimes our information sends us on a whole other platform. Still, sometimes, if we are willing to maintain our humility, it'll set us right back where we started.

Over the years, I've studied and veered into all sorts of different topics. Spiritual revelation is spiritual revelation, and it's always awesome to delve into different areas of thought and insight. So it would be safe to say that I've always enjoyed learning and expanding my horizons. I never thought much about it. Toward the end of my season, God started backtracking me to the very beginning of things I had taught and focused on in the early years of my ministry. When I say I went "back to basics," I went back to the very first things I ever studied and preached about. My foundations went back to the Kingdom, Christian identity in Christ, unity, even some of the apocryphal studies I did back then. I looked at things again, embraced them all over again, in the same way, in a new way, and with new eyes. It gave me whole new insight into those basics; to go over them once more and give them the glance they needed now.

Growing in God is great and yes, we should reach a point where we grow past the basics and are ready to take on more spiritually meaty things. It shouldn't be that we go over the same things year after year after year. I also can't deny that sometimes we need a reminder of the basics, of the things that started us off and got us going where we needed to be. God never promised us that the Christian life or walk would be easy. He never said the ministry would be a true breeze. That's why we need reminders of the basics: of those first teachings, promises, and foundations that set us where we are going. They prove to us that God is with us, and that those are the things that have set us on the path to be where we are now. We should build them and expand out, but we should never, ever forget them, or forget from where we've come.

Repeating the basics doesn't mean we've failed. It means we need to see them again in a new way, an enlightening way, an insightful way. There is always more to be learned about the basics: different insights, different perspectives, different shades and thoughts, different ways of looking at something, and of course, a deeper perspective, something that applies and makes sense for what we tackle and encounter right now. The basics are awesome, because no matter how advanced we get, we are reminded through them of the humility we find in Christ, and the power that He gives us to get us to each and every next step.

- Day 13 -
Just Upload the File Again!

WHATEVER YOUR HAND FINDS TO DO, DO IT WITH ALL YOUR MIGHT, FOR THERE IS NO WORK OR DEVICE OR KNOWLEDGE OR WISDOM IN SHEOL (THE PLACE OF THE DEAD), WHERE YOU ARE GOING.
(ECCLESIASTES 9:10)

READING: PROVERBS 13:1-10

ONE thing I learned during my season was handle the publication of my own books. For some time, I published magazines and small booklets, but for larger books, I had to depend on a much larger publisher. My experience with bigger-name publishers wasn't good. I wound up paying a large sum of money to someone who did not do their job. When the time came for the release, it was safe to say the book wasn't of the best quality. There were mistakes that shouldn't have been there. It wasn't promoted in the way it should. Thus, when the opportunity to handle the publishing came up, I was excited to launch our company into deeper waters and into new endeavors.

It's probably not a big secret to say the publishing industry has changed. Now we upload files to technical servers where they are scanned for issues that might make our books incompatible with printers. As a publisher, there's a great deal of technical considerations that go into publishing a book, far more than the average author takes into their thoughts. Once we've gone through the basic grammatical technicalities, we must consider page flow, space, font type, font size, page numbers, how text fits on a page, margins, and overall look as pertains to the form by which a book's pages fill out. Once it's time to upload the files to those servers, they have already been scoured for mistakes, a cover is designed (also scoured for mistakes and properly sized for the book's interior), and the waiting period begins as we discover what is what with the future printing of that book.

On one particular day, I was processing a book for a client that had turned into a great amount of work. Some books require more work than others, and this was one of those times when I had been through the book twice already to catch all the mistakes. It was one of those books that required extensive scanning and editing for mistakes, and I was ready to move to the next step. I was hopeful that it was ready to upload and was set to do it.

On the first upload, everything looked fine, except one minor spacing issue. Spacing issues are typically easier to pick up when looking at the file digitally, so I was fine with fixing it. No big deal. Then it said the cover was off. Then I tried to fix the cover again, and it was still saying it was off. By this point in time, I was ready to send a nice-nasty email to the printer and find out what they were complaining about, but instead I stepped back and said, "Just upload the file again, Lee Ann!"

Gee, now there's a novel concept. Just upload the file again.

Sometimes we spend so much time trying to fight what is or get around doing what we know we need to do that we waste energy and precious hours on nothing short of avoidance. We don't see the bigger picture, because our immediate sight rests on only the thing that's right in front of us – that which seems obvious. The problem is this obvious thing is often not a solution to the situation. If we just take the time to address what needs addressing, head on, we will save a lot of time and energy in the process. Yes, some things are decidedly more pleasant to deal with than others, but shouldn't those be the things we are just willing to address and move out of the way?

As an epilogue to the story, I did just what I said to do: I uploaded the file again. Only this time, when I uploaded it...it was fine.

- Day 14 -
You Can't Save Everybody

REMEMBER LOT'S WIFE!
(LUKE 17:32)

READING: GENESIS 19:1-28

WHENEVER we hear about or muse on the story of Sodom and Gomorrah, it's always in a limited context. People feel it is about something specific rather than something general that can apply to all believers. Truth be told, it is about something specific, but it is something specific that can apply to anyone and everyone, especially when we deal with someone in our lives that just seems to be headstrong about going their own way. Sure, we see it when we are working with people unto salvation. They don't want to give up this or that, because they fear doing so will change their lives too much. We expect it when it comes to those who are newly introduced to spiritual things from the perspective we present...but what about when it happens with those who claim to already be saved?

One of the hardest things I encountered in my season was coming to terms with the fact that believers can be as hard-headed and unresponsive to the move of God and His work in our lives as non-believers. As I watched those closest to me fall by the wayside, time and time again, it became more and more obvious that being headstrong is not a characteristic unique to unsaved people. It's something in all of us. It makes us stand back and realize in this work we'll have hits and we'll have misses, and there are some misses that we can't do anything about.

It was hard watching people who claimed to always be there or have my best interests at heart fall into patterns with others that were destructive or be led astray, so far astray they left and never returned. Some of them morphed into entirely different people than they had been prior. Seemingly sweet and unassuming people turned into viscous, venomous individuals set on destroying others. There were those who seemed dedicated to ministry who turned into disorganized, disinterested, and hostile people. All of a sudden, it was as if they became someone else, someone who was wild and undisciplined, and uninterested in hearing anything that questioned their way or their course. As a result, they went their own way, creating a trail of mess behind them. The rest of us remained, trying to figure out what was next. When people decide they are going to follow their own course, they forget about those who are left behind.

It makes me think of Lot as he stood in his city, a city where he lived for years, now suddenly forced to flee because indecency and wickedness took over to the point where there was no redemption. The people he knew, the friends he worked with, the people of the town now probably seemed radically different...and there was nothing he could do to change their course. There was nothing anyone could do, because they'd decided their fate for themselves.

Then there was Lot's wife. Not only did he lose his home and his friends, he lost her, too. Her decision to look back in longing over the life now gone meant she died along with it. He couldn't save her as she turned into a pillar of salt.

The truth is that none of us can save anybody; only God can do that. In the depth of our walk with Him, the misses we have, the people who leave, the ones who don't measure up quite as much as we might have hoped, remind us that the only One Who can truly save anyone is God. We can work with that, we can cooperate with it, we can assist with it, and we can be catalysts of salvation, but in the end, the only One Who saves is God. As we work with Him, some will come along, and some will not – but we always need to remember that we can't reach everybody.

- Day 15 -
Typical is Typical

AND WHEN THEY FOUND THEM NOT, THEY DREW JASON AND CERTAIN BRETHREN
UNTO THE RULERS OF THE CITY, CRYING, THESE THAT HAVE TURNED THE WORLD
UPSIDE DOWN ARE COME HITHER ALSO.
(ACTS 17:6, KJV)

READING: JOHN 15:16-23

IT wasn't until I reached the latter part of my season that I realized God wanted me to take a long, hard look at the state of my ministry so I could make some important changes. However, the message I needed to make changes started right at the beginning of the season, right out of the gate. The truth is if I look back in hindsight, we were a pretty typical, run-of-the-mill ministry. There wasn't anything real special or unique about us, save the fact that our ministry was noted by ethnic and racial diversity. We weren't the only ministry like this, however, even though I had the honor of being the first Caucasian woman to preach in many minority churches throughout the south. I would preach, I would teach, I educated people through our school, and I did some ordinations...but that was about it. On the surface, we looked like every other ministry out there that was competing for everyone's time and attention. For the most part, our ministry followers were from church backgrounds themselves, and I knew the topics to talk about – and avoid – to get the attention that was needed.

The problem with this is that it isn't what God told me – or anyone, for that matter – to do. There is nothing anywhere that says we should be typical, falling into a mold that has been pre-selected and established for us by others. As I started to deal with the reality that ministry had become a cookie-cutter endeavor, something we do to garner certain attention and get followers who are looking for something specific, I noticed it all around me. The way in which ministers speak, the way they know how to preach long and hard on certain sins, how to move their congregations and followers, and even how they know what to say to them personally and privately bespeaks to me a type, a pattern that we've evolved to make people find a familiar comfort therein. There's something comforting and reassuring for people as they know what to expect from their ministers. They expect a certain message and a certain slant to the passages they've heard preached over and over and over again. The problem with this is we take such comfort in the cookie-cutter ministry that we don't know how to respond to anything different or unique, and we are so opposed to having our comfort taken away, we don't receive anything different.

Typical ministry is typical ministry, which means it will bring forth a typical result. If all we are looking for is to keep comfortable people coming back to church every week, we'll be fine. The problem with this for any minister who is truly called is that they won't be content with keeping everyone comfortable. There will reach a point where the price to maintain the flow and keep everyone content and happy will feel too high, too unobtainable, and too boring. It will mean that minister keeps everyone where they are, no one grows, and things will happen that they will have to pretend they did not see and never address them.

For too long in my ministry, I kept everyone who followed it comfortable. I tolerated disrespect I should not have allowed. I didn't interfere enough in training processes and in the way ministries functioned. I preached things that didn't challenge because I knew if I did, I'd deal with the threat of never returning. Yeah, being typical has its costs, ones we can never think about. Even though we are not typical now, I would never go back. The price to be typical was just too high.

- Day 16 -
Embracing What You're Good at

WHATEVER MAY BE YOUR TASK, WORK AT IT HEARTILY (FROM THE SOUL),
AS [SOMETHING DONE] FOR THE LORD AND NOT FOR MEN,
KNOWING [WITH ALL CERTAINTY] THAT IT IS FROM THE LORD [AND NOT FROM MEN]
THAT YOU WILL RECEIVE THE INHERITANCE WHICH IS YOUR [REAL] REWARD.
[THE ONE WHOM] YOU ARE ACTUALLY SERVING [IS] THE LORD CHRIST (THE MESSIAH).
(COLOSSIANS 3:23-24)

READING: 2 TIMOTHY 2:1-8

I recently looked up the first pastor I ever had as a Christian. Because I am in the process of moving to a city where I last knew he was living, I was curious if he was still there. Turns out he's not there anymore, he was there to go to college for a bit. He then moved to the opposite end of the country. What took me aback most is that he isn't any longer in ministry. In fact, he's back doing the work he did before he was in ministry.

To say he and I didn't have the best relationship was an understatement. I was newly saved, very gung-ho about ministry, and he was arrogant. He liked being in control and the center of attention in the church. He was one of those pastors that we used to hear about in church hurt stories: aggressive, in-your-face, controlling. The church was definitely divided on his position of authority. When he announced he was leaving, the news was met with both joy and heartache. The transition to a new pastor didn't go over well with the church, it eventually split, and then this leader returned to the area to try and start a new church. In the long run, this endeavor didn't work out, but it worked long enough to divide the existing church he left behind, very much to its demise. I didn't know anything about him after he left our area again. It wouldn't be until a few years later I accidentally came across something of his online. He was now pursuing a book series which didn't do much, and a new community-based form of ministry, which also didn't work out. Then, fast-forward a few years later, he was back doing the work he did prior to his stint as a pastor and his later efforts of ministry.

Even in hindsight, he was not a very good pastor. He didn't exercise pastoral care in a way that conveyed he cared about people. I think he was a part of specific schools of thought that were customary and relevant given the specific time he rose to ministry in church, but those were on the downswing when he stopped pastoring the church I attended. The combination of what he felt he gave up, along with the specific theological training he'd received, made for a lethal combination. He was trying to gain something from ministry to make up for what he'd lost. In the process, he came across as an angry, hostile leader. In hindsight, given where I was and he was, it's no wonder we really didn't get along.

I'm glad to see that he found a place to be solid and successful in his life, even if it seems far removed from where he tried to be when I met him. The message in it for me is that it's so important we do and pursue what we are good at, and that we embrace what we are good at for ourselves. It's so common for us to try and pursue things that are just not the right fit, and to force those things to fit, even though they never do. Nowadays we think we should aspire to be in charge, to have rule over people, to lead others to a certain point in their lives, not considering whether such a position is for us. My former pastor took a role that was not for him to take, because being a pastor wasn't his true calling. What he is doing now is no less than pastoral work, it is just different. In its difference, he found his niche.

We think there's glamor in leadership; there isn't. There is hard work, which is what we find in any work or profession out there to which we might be called.

- Day 17 -
Hiding Behind Tradition

So for the sake of your tradition (the rules handed down by your forefathers), you have set aside the Word of God [depriving it of force and authority and making it of no effect].
(Matthew 15:6)

Reading: Mark 7:1-16

TODAY I plowed through a huge pile of papers that were a true blast from the past. Many of them were from at least six to eight years ago, long wrought between invoices, orders, and old letters. In the midst of the shuffle, I came across a "goodbye letter" I sent to a woman in ministry who I once considered a mentor several years back. We had one of those confusing interactions that revolved around her ever-changing life, including family issues and health problems. It ultimately fell apart, because no matter how much she got to know me, she was forever trying to change me.

We met through an internet radio podcasting site when it was still new. The network in those days was nowhere as big as it is now, and those who were faithful and consistent to broadcast became close-knit, knowing each other as friends. I was fascinated with this woman because people seemed so taken with her. People clambered to have her come to their church and felt she was so "anointed." People didn't take that way to me, at least not on the scale of this woman. I knew a few people who believed in the work and wanted to see it grow, but it was nothing like this woman had.

In hindsight, I understand it better now: she was

extremely traditional. She upheld concepts and traditions that were comfortable with the ministers she knew, and they encouraged her in that. She felt herself to be very right and very official, and nobody ever challenged her. She was confident that she was an ultimate authority. Instead of dealing with her echoes of tradition and focus on her methods that were quickly becoming outdated, she believed her methods to be right – and alternate ideas to be incorrect.

As I read the letter I sent her today, I concluded that her response to what I said to her was rather immature. I stated how she made me feel, I was able to prove that much of what she spoke over me did not come to pass, and that she owed me an apology for speaking down to me, as she frequently did. The letter wasn't written in hostility. I was surprised that seven years later, it wasn't as hostile as I remembered it being. Instead of admitting she was wrong and apologizing, she tried to trick me into receiving the letter with a rejection notice on it and deleted and blocked me all over the internet. I haven't a question in my mind that were I to find her today, I'd find her right where I left her.

When I left the Catholic Church in 1999, I really thought I was getting away from something. I thought the days of vain worship, arrogant leadership, and leaders who operate without God's anointing were over. I believed I would come into a place of seeing God in a different way and finally be able to work with people who weren't controlling and dominating, like I'd seen in my church of origin. What I have come to find (and could clearly see in the letter I found) is that what I saw in Catholicism, I still see, and battle, all these years later. The people might wear different outfits, but there are still people who hide their personal vanity behind tradition. It's a part of human nature: we want to be right. If we suspect we are wrong, we try to avoid that reality. Like it or not, tradition is tradition is tradition – whether it comes wrapped in a statue or in repetitive actions done to maintain our sense of power and control.

May we all pray to realize our traditions will keep us right where we are, year after year, as we insist we are right….when we aren't.

- Day 18 -
Impatients

CONSIDER IT WHOLLY JOYFUL, MY BRETHREN, WHENEVER YOU ARE ENVELOPED
IN *OR* ENCOUNTER TRIALS OF ANY SORT *OR* FALL INTO VARIOUS TEMPTATIONS.
BE ASSURED *AND* UNDERSTAND THAT THE TRIAL *AND* PROVING OF YOUR FAITH BRING
OUT ENDURANCE *AND* STEADFASTNESS *AND* PATIENCE. BUT LET ENDURANCE
AND STEADFASTNESS *AND* PATIENCE HAVE FULL PLAY *AND* DO A THOROUGH WORK,
SO THAT YOU MAY BE [PEOPLE] PERFECTLY AND FULLY DEVELOPED [WITH NO DEFECTS],
LACKING IN NOTHING.
(JAMES 1:2-4)

READING: JOB 6:1-21

I'M no stranger to finding people's abandoned or thrown-out items around my apartment complex. I don't exactly live in the Ritz Carlton of accommodation. In fact, the apartment complex where I currently live is pretty awful. It's not well-maintained. That means when people move out or decide to throw something away, they typically leave it near one of the complex dumpsters for a few days. This has led to some incredible finds, including a plant stand for my mom, a stack of old Watchtower publications all bound and printed spanning about a decade, a tote of old Happy Meal toys that entertained the children at the church, a potted yucca plant, and, most notably, a pot of impatients.

To be honest, I wasn't sure what was in the planter when it arrived at my house. I guessed a variety of different shrubbery plants, because they had no flowers and didn't look good. The pot they were in was severely cracked. As it was long after shrub plant season was over, I didn't expect them to last real long. Then, one day, to everyone's surprise, the plant got a bud. This confirmed it as a hot pink impatient plant, very much to my excitement. I had grown impatients at an earlier time, but I hadn't grown them for a number of years. Day after day, we would sneak outside to the porch to see it bloom. One bud appeared, then two, then three...and so on, as this plant presumed to be dead came back to life.

One day, my mom pointed out that the plant was there to hold a message. First, they are "impatients," which reflected the state of mind we all had at that time. It was a time when impatience was running high and patience was running low. Second, it was a plant that was left for dead, abandoned by its original owner, by a dumpster. Here it was, living and thriving, blooming and growing, even though someone else felt it was long gone. That was the place I was at: I assumed things were ready for the dumpster. Looking over the results of the season, too many had left things in the hopes they would die. The impatients proved it wasn't that easy, nor that simple, and where one sees death, someone else sees the potential for life. The impatient plant needed someone to take care of it properly. It needed the right help and support to survive and thrive, and the same was true for the circumstances we found ourselves in.

It's easy for us to get impatient in our seasons with God. We look at things and all we see is what we don't have. We don't see what God is trying to teach us, because we are too busy processing numerous feelings that cloud over the voice of God in our lives. Sometimes we must look at where we are and what's around us. There are times when we go through things that change us and those who've been with and around us are not qualified to handle where we are now and the help we need to get where we are going. This may sound cliché, but it is a hardened fact that doesn't change because we want to ignore our situation.

The impatients needed proper care. They needed the right people for the job, and they found us. The ministry I have needs proper care. I need the right people for the job, and one by one, God is bringing them to us. In the meantime, all we need is patience.

- DAY 19 -
Empty Momentarily, Die Daily

[I ASSURE YOU] BY THE PRIDE WHICH I HAVE IN YOU IN [YOUR FELLOWSHIP AND UNION WITH] CHRIST JESUS OUR LORD, THAT I DIE DAILY [I FACE DEATH EVERY DAY AND DIE TO SELF].
- 1 CORINTHIANS 15:31

READING: PHILIPPIANS 2:4-12

THROUGHOUT most of 2016, the *Power For Today* program was aired on a ministry-based internet radio station that didn't make it to the 2017 mark. The experience was great for me, because as I had been on and off radio for about ten years, I was personally approached, hand-selected, and given the opportunity to air the program for free. It wound up being a lot of work, but the program aired to reasonable success in that time frame. After a few months, I was asked to increase my programming presence, and begin new shows exclusively for them, as well.

The experience was interesting for me, because the ministry that aired my programming was decidedly conservative and traditional, and I am decidedly not either of those things. I suspected there was some undercurrent with my presence, especially when one of the producers (who later left the station) blocked me online, without stating a reason. My programs were some of the best-rated on the station, so axing me wasn't an option. Still, there were times when I suspected I was an oddity to the people who ran the station and they questioned my spirituality, because my presentation was so radically different from theirs.

There was no proof of this more evident than one day

when I started teaching in my Facebook inbox without any idea of what was to come out of my mouth. Every now and then, one of the founders would inbox me. Over that year, I heard a ton of messages or word directed toward me. Some of it sounded all right, some of it was way off, and some of it, I wasn't sure what it was or how to explain it. One day we were discussing books, talents, and abilities, in that literal order. It came up that I'd had a business partner at one time who left my company and was now doing work, on her own, that was both poorly done and a great example of the pride people have when they do not esteem themselves and their abilities properly. We all have different abilities and trying to have someone else's abilities or envying them is such a waste of time. No gift or ability is greater than another, and we all must embrace what we have and work with others so our end results are always better than we could ever accomplish by ourselves.

During the conversation, I made the statement: "Empty momentarily, die daily." The Bible tells us we die to ourselves daily. This doesn't mean we do something wrong every day, but it means we must constantly remember our position in Christ and humble ourselves before God. As He increases, the parts of us that like to hold on to our sense of control must decrease. We have to remember where we came from and where we are heading if we do not esteem ourselves properly and keep connected to the Father. In addition, in each situation that rises up and in every circumstance in which we find ourselves, we are forced to empty ourselves of our pride, of our stubbornness, of the things that keep us bound up and unwilling to admit our limitations. Moment by moment, with every little frustration, hostility, impatience, vanity, or egocentrism, we must empty ourselves of those things that keep us from achieving promise and purpose.

Empty momentarily, die daily. Consider everything we go through moment by moment and empty out the parts of us that need to change. Consider the call to become a new creature and die daily. Allow the two to transform, moment by moment, day by day.

- Day 20 -
Embracing My Inner (and Outer) Badness

BUT JAEL, HEBER'S WIFE, TOOK A TENT PIN AND A HAMMER IN HER HAND
AND WENT SOFTLY TO HIM AND DROVE THE PIN THROUGH HIS TEMPLE
AND INTO THE GROUND; FOR HE WAS IN A DEEP SLEEP FROM WEARINESS. SO HE DIED.
(JUDGES 4:21)

Reading: Luke 7:36-50

We've all seen the pictures of ministers dressed in flowing white robes or dresses as they hold up the Bible just below their perfectly made-up and dressed faces. There's never a hair out of place as they preach and move with what seems to be perfect poise, grace, and timing. They never misspeak or misstep, and the grandeur of their work seems to be noted by everyone. They are considered "good ministers," those who reflect what's considered to be the highest heights of heavenly revelation.

Being a "good minister" sounded like a good idea when I first went into the ministry, and I did everything possible to conform myself to this perfect image. After all, being "good" goes with the concept that we have of ministers. We are supposed to want to be good, and embody good, and think that being good represents a level of being prim and proper. This is especially true when it comes to female ministers, because we're always being told that we shouldn't want to "be like men." If a female minister is more comfortable teaching on doctrine or theology as opposed to fuzzy messages about healing or children's ministry, she is perceived to taking on a masculine role, and that role is somehow inappropriate or not suited for her. This also comes into play when women leaders take on heavier roles within leadership, including discipline or dismissal, and people feel they are somehow not acting feminine when they perform these tasks.

I've long studied gender identity and concepts of gender, and what I can say with a fair amount of certainty is this: there is no wrong way to be female. There is, however, a wrong way to be a leader, and it is wrong to treat people with kid gloves or to constantly ignore problems or weightier teaching because you don't want to be perceived as somehow being less feminine. In our pursuit to demean women, we now demean women leaders by criticizing a woman's ability to lead for no other reason than leading doesn't seem "ladylike" work.

I've come to a place over this past season where I am comfortable not being the embodiment of any type of woman that anyone feels I should be. I am here to be me, to be who God has created me to be, and that doesn't have a formal label. According to many people, I am not a "good woman," and I am certainly not a "good minister." I don't fit into the box people want to create, and that's fine. I am me; I am an apostle, I am the leader God has created me to be, I am not conservative, I am not perfect, I have my bad days, I even have moments where I utter things I shouldn't, and I am also not fake. You want a straight answer, you'll get one with me. If we look over the history of the Bible, most of the women therein haven't been "good women" and most of the ministers not "good ministers." They challenged their society, their notions, their ideals, and yes, even their theology, sometimes in the face of individuals who were far older than they were. They were world shakers, situation changers, and they didn't fit any mold or ideal shaped for them that might have existed in their day.

So yeah, I'm as bad as I have to be to get the job done. I'm not an angel; I'm a human being, down here in this day and age, who doesn't want to feel like I'm not measuring up because I am different. So here I shall sit, and occasionally put on my leather dress suit, show up, show out, and change the world.

- Day 21 -
...Why are You in My Life Again?

> NOW WHEN JOB'S THREE FRIENDS HEARD OF ALL THIS EVIL THAT WAS COME UPON HIM,
> THEY CAME EACH ONE FROM HIS OWN PLACE, ELIPHAZ THE TEMANITE AND BILDAD
> THE SHUHITE AND ZOPHAR THE NAAMATHITE, FOR THEY HAD MADE AN APPOINTMENT
> TOGETHER TO COME TO CONDOLE WITH HIM AND TO COMFORT HIM. AND WHEN
> THEY LOOKED FROM AFAR OFF AND SAW HIM [DISFIGURED] BEYOND RECOGNITION,
> THEY LIFTED UP THEIR VOICES AND WEPT; AND EACH ONE TORE HIS ROBE, AND THEY
> CAST DUST OVER THEIR HEADS TOWARD THE HEAVENS.
> (JOB 2:11-12)

READING: JOB 32:1-22

I suppose this is one of those if-you-have-to-ask-the-question-you-already-have-the-answer topics. We all have those times when we scan those we know and do those mental surveys as to where we're at and where they are at, but what do we do when we suddenly step back and see that one person who makes us go whoa...why are you here?

I already stated on an earlier day that when I came into my current season, I was what we'd call "typical." Along with me trying to be typical meant that I had a lot of "typical" people around me. They knew the typical way to speak, the typical events to have, and the typical things to say when I had an off day. For awhile, what they said and did worked. Maybe I should say it seemed like it worked. I had a lot more bad days back then and I was prone to intense ups and downs that seemed, at least on the surface, to be temporarily satisfied by the typical responses.

Then one day, God started pulling me out of the typical place where I was and the people who always seemed to be there had the same responses they'd always had on hand. The difference is their typical answers didn't work anymore. Suddenly, the people who seemed the most supportive seemed trite and disinterested. Over time, I started seeing them and their ministries differently, too. They didn't seem like the guiding stars they often appeared to be. They were just ministers, sometimes even just believers. They weren't as all-knowing or insightful as they might have claimed to be. They were people. I was a person. I needed a friend...and for this time, they were not able to be there.

The book of Job is a Bible volume that many believers could live without. Here was a guy, innocent as the day is long, who is suddenly faced with the most difficult trial of his life. The devil specifically picks on him because he's good, not because he's bad...and God lets it happen. God knew that Job could stand, so God let Job stand. Then over there were Job's friends, the people that were supposed to help Job through this time and comfort him, and encourage him to do right...right? Nah, Job's friends blamed him for what he went through. They thought he must have done something to miss God, and instead of helping him up, they made him feel worse.

It's important to note that the Bible refers to these people as Job's friends, not enemies. They were people who, at one time, shared their lives, their special events, their encouragement, and their prayers together. They were people who, prior to this incident, carried one another through difficult times,. Yet this experience was different, and it changed and challenged the relationships Job had with his friends. Through his experience, Job discovered what he was made of and saw the spiritual side of life in a radically different way than before. This means that everything looked and felt different on account of what he went through. It wasn't the same because he wasn't the same. His friends might have been fine at another time, but they weren't what he needed any more.

I can identify with this, because it is exactly what

happened to me. Sometimes the people we think will be with us forever are only there for a time. Once that time changes, the relationships change. There's nothing wrong with moving forward, but there is something wrong with keeping people around who have outlived their season.

- Day 22 -
Same Type of Crazy as Me

FOR JUST AS THE BODY IS A UNITY AND YET HAS MANY PARTS, AND ALL THE PARTS,
THOUGH MANY, FORM [ONLY] ONE BODY, SO IT IS WITH CHRIST (THE MESSIAH,
THE ANOINTED ONE).
(1 CORINTHIANS 12:12)

READING: PSALM 133:1-3

WHEN we go through periods of inner change, we feel the shifting paradigm within ourselves. It's an odd feeling that we often hope someone will come along and take away from us. All of a sudden, we are looking at situations we were fine and comfortable in with new eyes and...everything is uncomfortable. Not a little uncomfortable that might be easily changed with a little time or thought, but radically, unspeakably...uncomfortable.

Throughout much of my season, I was radically, unspeakably uncomfortable. I've gone through the different phases of feeling like there was something seriously wrong with me to coming out on the other side and adopting the mentality that God has taken me through this so I can embrace others who are the "same type of crazy as me." When we start out in ministry (at least when I started out) there was great emphasis placed on our ability to work well with others. We were encouraged to reach out, "network," "fellowship," and work with other ministers because it somehow proved our willingness to be a team player for the Gospel. So, for years, I would work with anyone who showed the least bit of interest in working with me. It took me a long time to realize that the ministry wasn't going anywhere. In my haste to work with others and prove myself willing to do so, I wasn't properly discerning and matching myself with others who shared my vision.

One day, I realized I needed to work with other people who are the "same type of crazy as me." There are so many people in ministry today to resolve or reconcile their own issues or to get attention, it can be difficult to truly step back and discern who to work with and who not to work with. It means that instead of jumping head-first into ministerial connections and relationships, we need to step back, take a discernment period, and pay special attention to the things people say and what they "give away" about themselves just by their speech patterns and the things they desire to share. Sometimes it means saying no, even to opportunities that might work out great for others. It means assessing every situation and discerning who – and what – is right to launch things into a greater place.

Unity is great, connection is great, and working with others is great. They are all nice concepts that I'm the first to admit need to be more than just concepts we embrace in theory but live in our lives. Yet unity isn't some nice musing that will just fall on our heads if we try hard enough or hope hard enough. If we aren't working with people who we can say with some assurance that we're on the same page within some way, we're just wasting our time. In church, we need to be willing to accept who we are, who God has created us to be, and find other people who are just as crazy to do the same in their lives and ministries. Just working "with anyone" is never a good idea, because there are so many things we don't ever know about others if we just take on anyone and everyone who crosses our path.

True unity reflects a deeper precept, one by which we know others, we care about others, and they are more than just random acquaintances who invite us to preach at their church, and then we return the favor. Crazy is as crazy does, and nowadays, God raises up the different so we can do a different work in the earth.

- Day 23 -
Right Down the Street, Under My Nose

KEEP ON ASKING AND IT WILL BE GIVEN YOU; KEEP ON SEEKING AND YOU WILL FIND;
KEEP ON KNOCKING [REVERENTLY] AND [THE DOOR] WILL BE OPENED TO YOU.
FOR EVERYONE WHO KEEPS ON ASKING RECEIVES; AND HE WHO KEEPS ON SEEKING FINDS;
AND TO HIM WHO KEEPS ON KNOCKING, [THE DOOR] WILL BE OPENED.
(MATTHEW 7:7-8)

READING: LUKE 2:42-50

MY textbook, *Introduction To Missions*, would not have been complete without a chapter reflecting the work of missionaries throughout the ages. One figure I was most excited to write about was Alopen. Alopen was the first missionary to reach China, long before anyone in the west ever considered it, somewhere in the 600s. He was a part of the Nestorian Church of the East, most likely a Syrian speaker from either Persia or the Byzantine Empire. His record is found on a tablet known as the Nestorian Stele, which records his journey and experience within China. By learning about Alopen, I also learned about the Nestorian Church of the East, most notably the differences between the eastern and western churches, all of which boils down to some minor differences in the perceived nature of the humanity and divinity of Christ. In modern society, it's not something we think much about. In the early centuries, however, groups spent their entire lives agonizing over these issues. Over time, these differences have caused the eastern and western churches to split, with many of the eastern churches retaining the ancient traditions of all our ancestors in the faith.

I knew when I read about the Nestorian Church of the East that it does, in some parts of the world, still exist that I wanted to see one of their services. I wasn't expecting anything amazing or outrageous, but a true preservation of something ancient, something otherworldly that I wouldn't likely see but once in a lifetime. So, I set out to find out how I could visit one of these churches. At the time, I wasn't very busy in ministry. I was waiting for my move out of the Raleigh area and our weekly service was temporarily on hold, pending the move. I had the time, I had the interest, and all I had to do was find a church that fit with the traditions of the Nestorian Church of the East.

My initial research was dismal. There were formal dioceses and organizations affiliated with this church, but they were all far away. Most were in the north and the western United States, and I was smack-dab in the middle of the southeastern states. I had no way to get to a Sunday service somewhere so far away. I certainly couldn't justify a trip to California just to visit a church, no matter how ancient it was. I gave up on the idea of seeing one of these services, keeping in mind that if I was somewhere one day that had one, I'd drop in and see what was up.

One night I was looking for different churches in the Raleigh area that would reflect different ethnic understandings of faith that are different from what we might typically see in western Christianity. I was dead set on visiting one church when I stumbled across a church that has Syrian roots, follows Syrian format, and is in communion with the Church of the East via India. This group of Christians, off the "St. Thomas Christians" of that area, trace their lineage back to the Apostle Thomas. Herein is the culture where the Gospel of Thomas originated, many of the legends around him, and around the work of the church. It wasn't where I expected it to be, somewhere distant and far away from me. Instead, it was right down the street, under my nose.

Sometimes the things we think we'll never see are right

in front of us, if we will only look for them. If we don't look, we won't find.

- Day 24 -
The Color of Favor

> BY THIS I KNOW THAT YOU FAVOR *AND* DELIGHT IN ME, BECAUSE MY ENEMY
> DOES NOT TRIUMPH OVER ME.
> (PSALM 41:11)

READING: GENESIS 6:1-8

MOST people assume the "color of favor" to be green, resembling that of money. They think the more money they amass, the more "favored" they are. Teaching over time has led us away from passages that prove good things happen to good and bad people alike. Materialism has nothing to do with how favored somebody might be. Favor is not a chance to amass a lot of stuff; it's an encounter with God, something by which we see God's hand at work in our lives. By favor, we see God in everything we do and everything we experience. God is there, whether it is something destined to work out the way we hope, or not. Sometimes He takes us right to what we need, and other times He takes us through to the end of a situation that we could have easily lived without.

Whenever I think of favor, I think of the color royal blue, for a few reasons. It's not my favorite color, but there's just something about it. Royal blue does signify royalty, even though it is often overshadowed by the color royal purple. It is also associated with tranquility, trust, and responsibility, which always brings me back to the trust and peace that we find in God. In the color blue, I think of the depth of a deep blue sky, the place that shows God's bounty, and reminds us of His throne in the heavens, which are far above the sky.

Throughout my season, the color royal blue happened to pop up whenever I was in a notably difficult situation and needed that reminder that God was with me. In one instance, it was a dress I wore for an ordination. At another, it was a dress I found at the store when I wasn't even looking. Another time, it was noting the deep royal blue color of a Bible I own and was using for a specific occasion. There was another time it was the color of my handkerchief for the day or a pair of shoes I was looking to buy. Time and time again, royal blue popped up and reminded me of God's presence in my life. It might not have felt like it, but He was working things out for my good.

I don't want anyone to take this super-literal as to assume I really believe favor has a specific color, because I don't. I think God reaches out to us as individuals and uses things we will easily identify to find Him in our everyday walk and reasoning. If we look over the history and experience of the Bible, it is something that happened quite often, as God reached out to different Biblical figures with visions, thoughts, and identifying points they could recognize quickly and say, "That's my God behind that!" In my instance, God used the color royal blue, reminding me of His favor on my life. Whenever royal blue pops up, there is the reminder of my royal inheritance in God, my good Father, my King, my protector, and my defender, even in the most difficult of situations.

I've heard people talk about favor from all different aspects: from that of obtaining jobs, spouses, money, cars, new houses, different things, and the endless debate as how "fair" favor is, or is not. Favor isn't a thing that's about earning; it's about relationship. It is a reflection of the relationship we have with God and the one He ultimately desires to have with us. God sends His favor in ways we can recognize, see clearly, and identify so at each and every turn, we will come to see Him at work in our everyday lives. It is His hope that we will never see Him as so distant so as to forget

He is as near as our next breath.

- Day 25 -
Just Do it

LOOK CAREFULLY THEN HOW YOU WALK! LIVE PURPOSEFULLY *AND* WORTHILY *AND* ACCURATELY, NOT AS THE UNWISE *AND* WITLESS, BUT AS WISE (SENSIBLE, INTELLIGENT PEOPLE), MAKING THE VERY MOST OF THE TIME [BUYING UP EACH OPPORTUNITY], BECAUSE THE DAYS ARE EVIL. THEREFORE DO NOT BE VAGUE *AND* THOUGHTLESS *AND* FOOLISH, BUT UNDERSTANDING *AND* FIRMLY GRASPING WHAT THE WILL OF THE LORD IS.
(EPHESIANS 5:15-17)

READING: LUKE 9:59-62

SOME women dream of the handsome prince coming into their lives to set everything perfect for them. Me, I dream of the perfect web tech to come into my life and take care of all my websites for me. Website design is not exactly my forte. It's actually something I'd rather not do. I have to use templates, and I openly admit to never figuring out how to use the software, beyond changing stuff that I find already pre-created. So, to me, my ideal, perfect person is a web designer who can come into my life and take over all the websites so they are done accordingly and I never have to think about them again.

I never imagined that so many years down the road, I would still have to take care of my websites myself. Doing them is a big chore. About once every four to six months, I set myself up to do updates. Updates aren't as big a deal as re-designing an entire site, so re-designs are reserved for once every year or two. Around the middle of last year, I started re-designs on every site I owned, and they weren't minor changes. Our entire sites were getting a makeover, and that included pictures and format as well as content. The entire process took weeks to complete. I finished all but one site, because I just wasn't sure what I wanted to do with it. Everything else was done, and done well, but there was still this one that remained and hung around...and I put off finishing it.

I didn't put off dealing with the website for one day or one week or even a month...I put it off for about seven months. By the time I got back to it, I wasn't even sure if I liked what I was doing with the site. I looked over the files and had trouble figuring out what I was aiming to do the first time around. So, I sat there...and thought about abandoning what I'd already done...and starting again...and then it came to me, clear as day: Just do it!

I've never been a big procrastinator, but I must admit that knowing I have website work to do is something I like to put off for as long as possible. That's because I know it's not my strongest point, and I would rather take my time and invest it in something else, something I can accomplish better or faster. Putting off the website work, however, doesn't change that it needs to be done, or how long it takes me, or how much work it is. It just makes it so it'll be a big, long project that must be completed some other day. Agonizing over it, changing it, making different decisions pertaining to it all are there to put off the inevitable and avoid doing what needs to be done because it's not something that I want to do.

I needed to just do the site and get it over with. The longer I waited, the longer I held up the needed progress. It was holding my business back and I needed to structure and fix my website so I could move forward with what I needed to do next. It was time to just do it – figure out what needed figuring out and move forward.

We're all waiting for some knight on a white horse to show up in some way in our lives. Whether it's a website, a spouse, a ministry opportunity, a job promotion, or something else, we all have hopes and dreams for something to come along that might seem to solve some problem we have. He might show up, or he might not. While we're waiting, let's stop putting off what we know we need to do and get it done, so we can move on.

- Day 26 -
Walking Around Naked

> AT THAT TIME THE LORD SPOKE BY ISAIAH SON OF AMOZ, SAYING, GO, LOOSE
> THE SACKCLOTH FROM OFF YOUR LOINS AND TAKE YOUR SHOES OFF YOUR FEET.
> AND HE HAD DONE SO, WALKING AROUND STRIPPED [TO HIS LOINCLOTH] AND BAREFOOT.
> AND THE LORD SAID, AS MY SERVANT ISAIAH HAS WALKED [COMPARATIVELY] NAKED
> AND BAREFOOT FOR THREE YEARS, AS A SIGN AND FOREWARNING CONCERNING EGYPT
> AND CONCERNING CUSH (ETHIOPIA), SO SHALL THE KING OF ASSYRIA LEAD AWAY
> THE EGYPTIAN CAPTIVES AND THE ETHIOPIAN EXILES, YOUNG AND OLD, NAKED AND BAREFOOT,
> EVEN WITH BUTTOCKS UNCOVERED—TO THE SHAME OF EGYPT.
> (ISAIAH 20:2-4)

READING: 2 CORINTHIANS 1:12-23

WHEN I discovered that God called Isaiah to walk around naked for three years, I was very glad we didn't live in Isaiah's day. I was not only relieved because I don't particularly desire to walk around naked, but also because I don't want to watch a bunch of people do it, either. I'm surprised nobody has thought of trying to use naked preaching as a unique plug to garner ministry attention. On second thought, maybe I won't pursue this line of thinking much further, because I don't want to give anyone bad ideas. Clothes are great, let's keep them on for preaching, and let us not lose sight of why God told Isaiah to walk around naked in the first place.

While we're on it, why did God tell Isaiah to walk around naked? It wasn't a statement against clothes or clothes as negative, so what exactly was it, and is it something that God wants to say to us today?

God commanded Isaiah to walk around naked as a sign of uncovering. The time was coming when the Assyrians would come in, take over Egypt and Ethiopia, and all the prisoners would be carried out into captivity, completely naked. His act of walking around naked was a political statement against the Assyrians, a warning to Egypt and Ethiopia as a sign of judgment and humiliation, and was a warning to Judah, because Judah's hope and expectation was in Egypt, rather than in God.

Isaiah's statement down the naked catwalk was probably not something most would have had in mind as a great way to get a message across. If we want to be taken seriously by great world leaders and people in power, we think the best way to accomplish that is to dress a certain way or carry ourselves in the same manner they do. We believe we can get attention by behaving in a manner parallel to others. If they come after us, we go after them, and so on and so forth. Isaiah's command to walk around naked, however, defies that precept. Instead of doing what they did, Isaiah did what nobody else would ever imagine doing: he became totally transparent. He bore it all for the sake of making others realize something very real was coming, and everyone needed to get themselves right because of what was to come.

Transparency is something I see as a great need for, especially in this season. I fully well admit to being someone who is on the private side, and sometimes I am not apt to share about my own thoughts or current experiences, because I know people are quick to judge. Isaiah reminds me we need to be transparent to bring about change, and true change only comes from those who are willing to be fully transparent. Transparency doesn't mean that we go airing out all our dirty business, but it does mean we are upfront and honest enough to show the world who we are, for real, and back it up with our viable experience.

Like it or not, God still calls us to "walk around naked," just with our clothes on. He still calls us to strip things down to the barest realities and reveal that which God requires of us. Isaiah's naked walk gives us a view of truth in its rawest, most uncomfortable, and most up-close-and-personal form, because truth starts with us.

- Day 27 -
Distractions

LET THE WORDS OF MY MOUTH AND THE MEDITATION OF MY HEART BE ACCEPTABLE
IN YOUR SIGHT, O LORD, MY [FIRM, IMPENETRABLE] ROCK AND MY REDEEMER.
(PSALM 19:14)

READING: LUKE 10:38-42

I first got word on distractions and the command to be focused for a New Year's message I issued about three years ago. I talked about the way we are notably distracted in the church today and attributed that distraction to the fact that the enemy knows he can throw anything he wants any which way, and we'll run wild, chasing after it. We haven't learned the power of concentration, focus, and discipline in our lives; thus distraction is the major way the enemy gets our attention and engages us to the point where we will not do what we should do if we are constantly distracted.

The key to distraction is the thing the enemy uses to get our attention. If we have big enough family problems or so many small ones we can't pay attention, that's what he throws our way. If it's disappointment with ministry, that's what he will use. Whether it's health issues or emotional problems, they show up on our doorstep. Time and time again, if they are what he thinks he can use to get a solid rise out of us, they will keep coming up, over and over again. The more we run after them, the more we will see those problems crop up. Because the distractions seem like things we must answer right now with total immediacy, we think we must answer them so we can move past them. The problem with this: following these problems doesn't solve them. When one is resolved, another one pops up.

Not too long ago, I started looking around at different people I know and how distracted they still are. Even though I have taught on distraction before and it's not uncommon to hear a minister or preacher encourage their church or ministry to stop being distracted, we don't tell people how to do that. We tell them to focus, but we don't tell them how to do that. All we do is throw around some staunch words, some ideas that assume those who are listening know how to do what we are telling them to do.

Truth is, we don't know how to focus (at least not very well) because we look at distractions incorrectly. When something distracts us, we think we should stop what we are doing and address the distraction, so we can remove it. We give all our time and attention to the distraction, because we think it won't go away if we don't. Once the distraction is gone, we think our lives will return to normal and our focus on where it should be. We think the only way we can focus is if a distraction is not there, so we set ourselves to remove the distraction. By doing this, we take our attention away from where it should be and place it squarely on the distraction. When whatever distracts us resolves itself, we then assume we'll go back to proper focus, but it never lasts long. It lasts as long as a distraction-less life continues (which is never very long) and then we start focusing on the new distraction that pops up at what feels to be the most inopportune time. When we handle problems like this, we never get to the point where we move beyond distractions to real work.

Focus is the ability to pay attention and concentrate on that which one is assigned to do. When we give our focus to eliminating distractions, we'll keep being distracted. Instead of getting rid of distractions, we need to focus on our assignments despite distractions. Sometimes that means saying no, sometimes it means ignoring issues, sometimes it means letting someone else handle things, and sometimes it means praying through and allowing life to go on while you do your work.

- Day 28 -
I Can't Do it With You – But I Can Still Do it!

JESUS GLANCED AROUND AT THEM AND SAID, WITH MEN [IT IS] IMPOSSIBLE,
BUT NOT WITH GOD; FOR ALL THINGS ARE POSSIBLE WITH GOD.
(MARK 10:27)

READING: PHILIPPIANS 4:10-13

SABOTAGE. There's a word we don't like to hear, especially when we talk about church. We think everyone is supposed to be all nice and Barney-song-like, spreading rose petals at our feet as we venture to do what God tells us to do. Maybe we don't think of it in this extreme, but there is a general consensus that when we undertake something spiritual, we assume others will be there to help us and want to be a part of it. In turn, we are supposed to be there to help them, too. It sounds ideal, very Christian and purposed, and the best way to get things done.

If it sounds so good and we all agree it's a good idea, why can't we ever seem to make this system manifest?

It's no secret that I've seen many people come and go through the duration of my season. Those who left felt leaving would make some sort of a statement against me and the work, unto its demise. Maybe they didn't expect the whole work to tank, but they did think they were important enough to thwart things and make them very difficult. It wasn't enough to look around at many who remained and realize there were a few in the bunch who reached a point of sabotage. They might have liked me well enough, but they were going to hold fast to whatever they felt needed doing or what was most important and do nothing to go out of their way to be helpful. The day came when I realized I was being better supported by those outside of my ministry than those who were supposed to be an up-close part of it. It didn't mean I couldn't do ministry; I just couldn't do it with those I'd been working with, even if they'd been with me for some time.

Unity is not something that comes and goes, although we definitely treat it that way. We always hope our assistance in a project can wait until the timing is more opportune or we feel better about things. This all relates to unity. Every time we manipulate the strings of unity, we break faith with others in the Body. We use our assistance (or more than likely, the idea of our assistance – whether it's time, support, participation, or financial) as a weapon to make sure someone else can't move ahead of us or advance. We make others feel bad, like they can't do something because we don't care enough to get behind them.

The thing I've learned in the midst of all this passive-aggressive and rather fleshly reality is simple: no, I can't do it with you. In fact, if this is who you are, I don't want to do this project with you, let alone any other project. You don't believe in me enough to give of your time, participation, finances, or attention, and that's fine. It means we aren't in unity, we never were in unity, and we aren't sharing the same faith that encourages both of us to move from selfish places by which we are dominated by the flesh to new levels in Christ. No, I can't do it with you, but that doesn't mean I can't do it at all. I can still do it; you just won't be a part of it.

There's a part of us that gets comfortable and dependent upon those who claim to want to help. Our focus is often on those people rather than on God, Who has the power to bring new people, new support, new finances, and new help into our lives. We grow to rely on others and think if they go away, we can't get it done. Whatever you are doing, you can do, no matter who is there to help, or not. No, we can't do it with saboteurs, but we can do it without them, better than we've ever imagined.

- Day 29 -
Becoming Foolproof

FOOLS MAKE A MOCK OF SIN *AND* SIN MOCKS THE FOOLS [WHO ARE ITS VICTIMS;
A SIN OFFERING MADE BY THEM ONLY MOCKS THEM, BRINGING THEM DISAPPOINTMENT
AND DISFAVOR], BUT AMONG THE UPRIGHT THERE IS THE FAVOR OF GOD.
(PROVERBS 14:9)

READING: PSALM 119:123-132

WHEN we had church in Raleigh, North Carolina, our weekly Bible study was always on Wednesday nights. One particular evening, our Bible study turned into a supportive counseling session for one of our members. It was one of those nights where the men didn't show up and it was just "us girls." One member needed particular encouragement and help for an issue she'd experienced earlier that day. When it came down to the long and the short of the conversation, the end assessment of the discussion was a need to "become foolproof." We all realized how many times we've succumbed to the wrong people or wrong ideas, and that doing so often comes down to discernment. When we are in situations and we read them wrong or assess them incorrectly, we wind up in messy circumstances. When we go through these circumstances, we are supposed to learn from them. The ultimate goal is to read the situations appropriately and, in the process, become foolproof.

When we talk about the "gift of discernment" in church, we skirt over what it is and how it works. I've come to define discernment as "the gift of knowing better," because that's exactly what it is. It's having the ability to look at a situation and see beyond the immediate into the long-term and eternal results. The spiritual aspect of discernment is identifying the spirit behind such a situation. Sometimes things can seem one way on the surface but seem completely different when we start looking at them from the perspective of underlying motive. As a general rule, none of us deliberately goes into situations with the intent or desire to be fooled and reap a mess. Nobody likes dealing with such aftermath, so we don't go into such situations expecting to find such. When deception is involved in a situation, the underlying spirit is dishonest, intending to make sure we think things are on the up and up, even though they are not. If the purpose is to deceive, that means we need true spiritual insight to assess a situation and to avoid deception. To exercise this gift means falling into a few situations that require our discernment muscles to strengthen and grow. We might miss the mark, but that only helps us to know what we should do for next time.

As people, we are hard on ourselves. We look back over situations with the lens of our hindsight and think we should have known the warning signs we now recognize. It's simplistic to say discernment comes about with experience, but the reality is that it does. In each situation we face, we must learn to recognize the leading of the Spirit to what underlines everything we see. The more we exercise our gift, the more we discern situations faster and with less hassle and heartache. The more we experience discernment, the less we will be fooled by our enemies in this world.

We are all imperfect. We are all flawed. We've all trusted the wrong person, walked head first into the wrong circumstances, gotten into the wrong situation, and attached ourselves to bad things that led us down wrong paths. We're all learning, and that should give us hope. The more we learn, the more promise there is for a future where we are more foolproof. Instead of being frustrated by the process, we should rejoice in the hope of a learned experience. That way, we focus on victories that lead us to better places as we grow in Him.

- DAY 30 -
Is God Busy Watching Karachi?

ARE NOT TWO LITTLE SPARROWS SOLD FOR A PENNY? AND YET NOT ONE OF THEM WILL FALL
TO THE GROUND WITHOUT YOUR FATHER'S LEAVE (CONSENT) *AND* NOTICE.
BUT EVEN THE VERY HAIRS OF YOUR HEAD ARE ALL NUMBERED. FEAR NOT, THEN;
YOU ARE OF MORE VALUE THAN MANY SPARROWS.
(MATTHEW 10:29-31)

READING: PSALM 8:1-12

EVER since VICELAND launched as a television channel on my cable package in mid-2015, it is usually what's on during the day (and sometimes at night). The channel offers viewers into the world of literal up-close-and-personal reality, showing firsthand what is going on in different communities around the world every day. It's not news reporting like we are accustomed to seeing; it is something different. It's documentary-style reporting on real life, the things people are experiencing and dealing with, in a way that I've never seen on television before. The topics range from eating pizza in New York City and fashion's impact upon a culture, to serious topics such as female genital mutilation and rental abuses existing in certain parts of the world. No matter who you are or what interests you, this channel opens the world to you in a new and unexpected way.

One thing that shook me to the core was hearing the populations of some cities in different countries. In the United States, we think a city is "large" if it has a few million people in it. In other countries, major cities have massive, ridiculous population densities. In Karachi, Pakistan for example, the population is approximately 25 to 30 million people alone.

That's in one city, and that one city has the same approximate population as the state of Texas. In one city, they have more people than we have here, in an entire state! It's no wonder they have issues with infrastructure and governance. How in the world can the government of one city maintain the needs of such a large population? It can't, and the results are corruption, severe poverty, sanitation issues, and crime.

The major thing such a high population density makes me consider is how does God do it? Sometimes when things aren't going well for me, I step back and wonder if maybe God is busy watching Karachi. We have one God and all these billions of people on the planet, and it's an amazement to me that things keep functioning day to day. The sun rises and sets, we don't all spin off into the black abyss of the universe, and life maintains its semblance of usual course, even though billions and billions of people exist.

It should be duly amazing to us that we have a God Who, as our Creator, isn't standing back and ignorant to our issues or problems. The same God Who hears the needs of people in a city like Karachi is the same God Who multitasks His time so well, He can attend to our thoughts and needs halfway around the world, as well. There's nothing too big or too small for Him, and the evidence of that can be found in the world's massive population. He does for us, just as He does for the next one.

Even though we do not always get what we want from God, He does hear us. He considers our thoughts and needs as well as our circumstances, all of which factor into His responses to our prayers. It might not be the response we hope for, but it is always the one we need, right in due time. Some of the darkest and most frustrating hours of our lives are the times when we need to wait on God, trusting in Him when we don't understand, and standing on faith that He does hear us and is never too busy watching Karachi to hear our prayers.

Although heaven knows, someone needs to be busy

watching Karachi.

- DAY 31 -
The Man Upstairs

I THANK MY GOD IN ALL MY REMEMBRANCE OF YOU. IN EVERY PRAYER OF MINE
I ALWAYS MAKE MY ENTREATY *AND* PETITION FOR YOU ALL WITH JOY (DELIGHT).
(PHILIPPIANS 1:3-4)

READING: NUMBERS 6:22-26

MOVING into my current residence was not by choice; it was out of necessity. I'd lived in my prior apartment for three years and it had serious drawbacks, but it had a nice layout and was relatively roomy for an apartment. Then a new company came in and the rent started going up…and up…and up. then income changed, forcing me to move. The apartment I found was good for what I was able to find within the price range needed, but it was a definite step down from where I was living. It didn't help that the move-in process was awful, the appliances and apartment were generally unclean and having to start over in a place that seemed like a downturn from where I was wasn't a pleasant experience. I took a deep breath and resolved to start again.

The man who lived upstairs from me lived in the apartment complex for a few years before I arrived. I never knew his name; to me, he was always "the man upstairs," someone I would greet when he was outside and occasionally complain about the situation with the complex when he was ready to talk. He was frequently on his balcony because he had a nasty smoking habit, so he was out there often and became quite a fixture in our neighborhood. As with most people, he kept to himself. He was a decent neighbor, relatively quiet, clean, and no problem whatsoever, as a general rule.

When my mom moved down to North Carolina from New York, she immediately took a liking to my upstairs neighbor. She had always been very friendly with strangers and liked talking to neighbors. Every time she was outside at the same time as the man upstairs, they would talk. They both shared an interest in plants and would talk about the different ones he had on his porch, and we had on our porch. When he watched a dog for a friend, we would come and talk to the dog. He grew to like my two dogs, as well. I didn't know a lot about him, but I came to take his presence above us for granted as we went about our days.

Then the day came when he announced he was moving out. After three and a half years of having him as my upstairs neighbor, I was upset. You never know who you'll get in an apartment situation, and I have spent plenty a night spraying bug spray outside because someone obviously had creatures in their apartments. More than anything else, however, I had gotten used to his presence. There was something comforting and familiar in having him around. I knew things were all right as long as he was there.

His parting gift to my mom was a Mandevilla plant that I'd fallen in love with and several assorted pots, all because he didn't want to move them. Now looking at those things reminds me of that same reassurance. This isn't where I ever wanted to live, but it's where I am. Things are going to be all right, no matter how hard they might get. It might not be ideal, but there is comfort and reminder in everything that remains from his time as my upstairs neighbor.

Man upstairs, if you read this, I hope you are enjoying your new apartment. I don't like the new people who moved upstairs. You were a far better neighbor than they will ever be. We are taking good care of your plant (it's absolutely beautiful!) and getting use of your pots. I miss our occasional talks.

Oh yeah, and thanks for everything.

- Day 32 -
Surprises

FOR THE VISION IS YET FOR AN APPOINTED TIME AND IT HASTENS TO THE END [FULFILLMENT];
IT WILL NOT DECEIVE OR DISAPPOINT. THOUGH IT TARRY,
WAIT [EARNESTLY] FOR IT, BECAUSE IT WILL SURELY COME; IT WILL NOT BE BEHINDHAND
ON ITS APPOINTED DAY.
(HABAKKUK 2:3)

READING: PSALM 130:1-8

WAITING to move is never fun, but it becomes a lot less fun when you are still waiting to move after two lease renewals. It's understandable at first, but when your life is on hold month after month, and things don't seem to change or go according to plan, life becomes a little on the confusing side. Should I pack? What should I pack? What will I need to leave out? What do I need to have first access to? What might I need right now? Where is my stuff? Why am I moving? Why did I ever pack this?

...And the list goes on and on, in what feels like an endless parade of mess. Boxes everywhere, not knowing where things are, being uncertain of what to pack and then wondering where something is, and waiting...all tend to take their toll after a while.

That's where I found myself. My lease was up in July; it was renewed. Then it came due for renewal, again, and things still weren't tied up. Moving still wasn't the option I'd hoped it would be, because there was nowhere to move. I had a city, I had a general direction, I knew what to do once I got there, but here I was, still waiting and still sitting. The sitting was boring, not moving forward was frustrating, and navigating through the few boxes I'd packed that now sat in my small, overcrowded apartment was aggravating. I'd gotten the word on God about moving, and now all I wanted to do was move.

The funny part about it all was that when I first got the word about moving, I wanted no part of it. I was accustomed to where I'd been living for the past eight years, and I didn't want to have to acclimate to a whole new city. That initial feeling of inward protest eventually passed to seeing the real need for a new start and a new change. Having to acclimate to another city seemed a small price, and my discontent with where I was started to grow. So, the days turned into weeks and the weeks months, and despite looking for a place to live regularly (which was the only hang up), there was nowhere yet to move.

So, when I was asked if I found anything one day, I was honest about it. No, and at the moment, there was nothing available through the agency I was working with, and that wasn't a matter of it being about price. There wasn't anything available, period. The woman I spoke to understood what I meant. It's hard believing and trusting for something and not seeing anything when you look around. She told me something would turn up, and even though the wait was hard, it makes it that much more special when it finally materializes and everything comes to pass.

I must admit, she had a point I never thought of before. Sometimes we look around at everyone else and their movements and feel like we're getting left behind. It's easy to think that everyone is moving on, even though there are plenty of people in our same situation, waiting on God to move for them, even if we don't see it that way in the natural. As the world moves around us and people come and go, the specialness of what is to come gets lost in the wait. All we want is our wait to end, with no thought or consideration for what we are waiting for.

There is something as special in waiting as there is in receiving. In waiting, we have the anticipation of receiving what is to come and watching God bring it to pass.

- DAY 33 -
Ain't Nobody Got Time for That!

SO TEACH US TO NUMBER OUR DAYS, THAT WE MAY GET US A HEART OF WISDOM.
(PSALM 90:12)

READING: HOSEA 10:7-12

IF there is one thing I dislike, it's wasting time. Time is the one thing we all have that finds a way to quickly get away from us in our lives. Once it's gone, we can never get it back. Because I dislike wasting time, I considered myself to be a pretty good student of its usage. I was good at scheduling, staying on task, staying close to planned schedules, and with completing things, but there was one way that I wasted time, and I never even considered it: I was good at wasting time on things that didn't matter and were not that important.

When I first started walking in the office of the apostle out loud and in color, I was trained by a leader who was brilliant in scholarship, but lousy with people skills. She was always getting into fights, especially online. It was her custom to teach people who didn't particularly care to be taught, and the result was frequently disastrous. It was her belief, however, that her methods were productive. She felt that argument still opened the door for dialogue, and it invited ideas and concepts to those who otherwise would never receive them.

The one flaw in her theory – which I must admit, sounded good at the time – was that these people who would never receive the concepts were still not receiving them. They were just having a big fight over ideologies and nobody walked away any wiser. They would fight and argue to the complete termination of the concept and any chance of ever having relationship with one another. Therein also lies the reason why the whole mess never amounted to much: they were people without relationship. She had appointed herself as their teacher, as someone to bring something to them, but she did not have any sort of relationship with them. They never decided she was their leader or teacher; thus, she was trying to teach them, and they had no interest in her.

I picked up on this very poor teaching method because I didn't know there was another way to handle things. I spent hours online, arguing with people to no avail and no purpose. My ideas might have been good, but my presentation was poor enough that others didn't receive it through that method. Through my argumentation, I thought I would be noticed, and people would see things differently. In the end, nobody changed their minds. We sat and argued, the other party would get mad and block me, and we would all go about our lives like the event never happened.

When God started dealing with me about the number of hours I wasted with this improper discussion method, I was ready to receive His instruction, but it still wasn't easy. Breaking the habit of being literally obsessed with who said what, who responded how, who thought what, and who said what against who had become a lifestyle based on bad teaching and lack of impact. It took time, but I broke the habit. Once I did, it became glaringly obvious to me how much time we waste on nothing. We pursue people who aren't interested, we start fights over things that don't need to be a fight, and we don't show proper respect where it's due. There is a better way to do things – both in teaching and disagreement.

All of us need to step back and look at the things we do and instead of chasing every wind of everyone, say to much of it, "Ain't nobody got time for that!" Focusing on what matters is what makes a difference. Attend to the people, places, things, and ideas that make that difference – and leave the haters to God.

- DAY 34 -
Small Wonders

SO TEACH US TO NUMBER OUR DAYS, THAT WE MAY GET US A HEART OF WISDOM.
(PSALM 90:12)

READING: 1 CORINTHIANS 1:27-31

I have played Facebook games since they first became available. Starting with the original Farmville, I always found social outlets and solace in game playing. I have always kept it to a limit, and any time it started taking up too much time in my days, I would always cut back. The few free games I play on a regular basis help me to unwind and process my days properly. I receive some of my best thoughts while playing an online game because the game requires me to focus and pay attention to what I am doing in a way that I can't when it comes to our everyday business. I've been known to sit up, sometimes late in the night, just to take a little time and play a game that demands my focus.

The current game I play incorporates all my favorite aspects of the free game world. It contains hidden objects, match three, mine sweep, matching, and different levels of identifying the different objects in the image. Sometimes I am looking for shapes, sometimes the words are jumbled, sometimes I must look for matches, and so on. There are so many ways the game is challenging and different. I have grown to love to play the game I play now for this very reason.

I love to play it, but I hate to lose, especially when I am running out of energy. I refuse to spend money on the game. That means when I'm done with energy, I am done, and that I have to work pretty hard to get the bonuses and other things that many pay for once they start playing. Sometimes I just don't want to have to play a level again or look for the same things once more, so I started praying when I have those moments. I ask God to help me find whatever it is I am looking for or to complete the puzzle at hand, and I have done so with amazing results. Any time I pray about finding something or finishing something when I play my game, I always meet with success.

This interests me from a spiritual perspective because in the scope of the universe, playing my game is not that important. A game is certainly not the focal point of my whole day. When I look back over my life, it will certainly not stand as something particularly memorable in and of itself. It isn't life or death, and it certainly isn't something that really matters. Whether I want to complete that puzzle or not, my life will go on if I don't. It's not something I'll lose sleep over. Yet God cares enough about me to pay attention to this little thing in my life. He hears when I ask Him to help me, and in this small way that might be insignificant to some, He proves He is always with me.

I think we've been taught in our current church settings to chase after big signs and moments of God's presence. Big signs can be great and lead to great things, but they aren't the only ways God moves. We think God needs to show up and show out all the time, and we forget that whether we realize it, God is always with us. It's not wrong to believe God can do big things, but sometimes I think we are overlooking the smaller things because they aren't grand enough or showy enough for our personal hopes and tastes. Maybe instead of looking for major moves, we should take comfort in the small wonders God surrounds us with to make us aware of His presence in a different sense from that which we often chase. God wants us to know He is always there, always concerned, and never too far away for us to find Him in our everyday lives. It's the small wonders that teach us this lesson, front and center.

- Day 35 -
Things Have Got to Change

BRING FORTH FRUIT THAT IS CONSISTENT WITH REPENTANCE [LET YOUR LIVES PROVE YOUR CHANGE OF HEART]; AND DO NOT PRESUME TO SAY TO YOURSELVES, WE HAVE ABRAHAM FOR OUR FOREFATHER; FOR I TELL YOU, GOD IS ABLE TO RAISE UP DESCENDANTS FOR ABRAHAM FROM THESE STONES! AND ALREADY THE AX IS LYING AT THE ROOT OF THE TREES; EVERY TREE THEREFORE THAT DOES NOT BEAR GOOD FRUIT IS CUT DOWN AND THROWN INTO THE FIRE.
(MATTHEW 3:8-10)

READING: MATTHEW 3:1-7

FOR at least four years, I hallowed the words "Things have got to change!" at the end of every year. My standard statements always consisted of the following: "I can't have another year like this year!" "We have got to do something different!" "I do not want another year like the last one!" "I can't just keep going on like this!" It was a hallowed tradition that, after two or three years, started to get on my nerves. When I realized I was saying the same thing and then doing the same things to inhibit change, I got annoyed. It didn't make any sense to try and herald change if I was going to do the same things, and that was exactly what I was doing. I was talking about change and expecting change to come to me as if it is some sort of magical fairy dust that makes everything better in life. When it didn't magically appear, I'd just resume life as I did the things I always did prior. As a result, change never came.

Then when I did actually recognize my behavior and start to make changes, it wasn't as simple as I imagined it would be. For one, it didn't feel as good as I hoped it would; it felt like work. There were so many things that needed doing, I didn't know where to start. I would start with one thing and then change would be required somewhere else, and it felt like a never-ending cycle. It didn't feel good or positive. It felt like...change.

The more changes I made, the more conflicts I discovered. There were people who claimed to feel just fine about one thing but quickly change when confronted with it. Change changed everything: it changed my life from the bottom up; it changed who I perceived my friends to be; it changed who I was able to work with, and who I was not. Change is change is change, and that means when we call for it...things change.

Change is one of those questionably dirty words because it's something we say we want, but it's amazing how often we avoid it when it becomes reality. We avoid it for all the same reasons and results I spoke of earlier: it means our friends change, how we feel about our life changes, and all of a sudden, we don't find ourselves in as comfortable or content of a place as we did once upon a time. We like the idea of advancement and forward movement, but we don't think about the price we will have to pay to have those things. Moving forward, advancing, and getting to a place where we don't have the same issues anymore means leaving the things and people behind who aren't constructive for change. It's great to think our lives are going to be easy and that change will fix everything around us that needs fixing, but change is a process. It is that series of steps, those various stages that come along and demand we do things differently than we have done them before. Praying for change doesn't mean God comes along and magically transforms everything around us. It does mean He will open our eyes to the things we are doing and to the things done in our immediate environment, so we know what to do differently.

We all pray for change, but the realities of change remind us to be careful what we pray for. Yes, change is great in the end, but until the end comes, it's challenging work. This is because change is choice.

- Day 36 -
The Rosy Color of Hindsight

AND THE MIXED MULTITUDE AMONG THEM [THE RABBLE WHO FOLLOWED ISRAEL FROM EGYPT] BEGAN TO LUST GREATLY [FOR FAMILIAR AND DAINTY FOOD], AND THE ISRAELITES WEPT AGAIN AND SAID, WHO WILL GIVE US MEAT TO EAT? WE REMEMBER THE FISH WE ATE FREELY IN EGYPT *AND* WITHOUT COST, THE CUCUMBERS, MELONS, LEEKS, ONIONS, AND GARLIC. BUT NOW OUR SOUL (OUR STRENGTH) IS DRIED UP; THERE IS NOTHING AT ALL [IN THE WAY OF FOOD] TO BE SEEN BUT THIS MANNA.
(NUMBERS 11:4-6)

READING: DEUTERONOMY 8:1-10

ALL of us stand at crossroads in our lives and reflect on our past situations differently. Most of us see things with differing levels of clarity in hindsight. This has led to the expression, "hindsight is 20/20." In other words, people believe that looking back on memories is going to be perfectly clear and bring perfect insight into whatever you went through before. But is it true that hindsight is really 20/20? Does time bring perfect insight and vision into what we went through in the great beyond?

It's true that in looking back, we might discover things we didn't notice while we were going through situations. When we are in the throes of things, we are also in the throes of feelings and emotions, and those emotions tend to cloud over our better judgment. In states of hurting, anger, or emotional stress, all we want to do is avoid those feelings. As a result, situations can seem much more intense and difficult than they might otherwise. Circumstances are never easy, nor real deep or insightful, when we must deal with them. It's easy to be caught up in the hope of finding a resolution, rather than genuinely stopping and seeing what God might be speaking in that specific situation.

When situations are over, we are usually going through or dealing with something else. We might get a temporary reprieve, but most of our lives are spent dealing with difficult things and figuring out how to overcome other things. When we face our past considering the things we deal with now, our past might not seem as difficult as it did then...it might even seem easier. It might even seem like what we had in our past was more desirable than we have now, and we might want to go back to it.

One day, a while ago I was reading about the Israelites in the wilderness. I suddenly realized how absurd some of the things they said were, considering they were slaves. Things didn't go their way, and now they were sitting around remembering garlic, onions, leeks and melons. Who in the world remembers those things? Garlic, onions, leeks and melons are certainly not points of 20/20 hindsight and clarity. If that's the highlight of your memories, what was your reality like? All of a sudden, slavery was worth garlic, onions, leeks, and melons because they weren't getting their way in the wilderness.

The Israelites prove to us that hindsight isn't 20/20 – it's rose-colored. It has the rosy hue of nostalgia, of the times we had way back when. Considering what we go through right now and what is to come, the past probably seems different. Mostly it will seem easier, and it will seem like what we had back then is something we should aspire to have right now. The problem is things won't be the same, because we aren't living in "way back when" anymore. We're living in now, with new challenges and ideals. In an ideal world, things should seem easier in hindsight because we aren't living them anymore. We've advanced beyond our past and our memories. Yes, they are going to seem different now than they did before. That doesn't mean what we are going through now is any harder to tackle than anything we experienced prior, because in those days, we were on a completely different level.

- DAY 37 -
I'm not on Clearance!

BECAUSE YOU ARE PRECIOUS IN MY SIGHT AND HONORED, AND BECAUSE I LOVE YOU,
I WILL GIVE MEN IN RETURN FOR YOU AND PEOPLES IN EXCHANGE FOR YOUR LIFE.
FEAR NOT, FOR I AM WITH YOU; I WILL BRING YOUR OFFSPRING FROM THE EAST
[WHERE THEY ARE DISPERSED] AND GATHER YOU FROM THE WEST.
(ISAIAH 43:4-5)

READING: ROMANS 5:8-13

It all started when I posted a status on Facebook. I received an inbox from someone I hadn't heard from in ages. The individual in question was one I had considered myself friendly with once upon a time, but that time had long since passed. He had told me he wanted me to speak at a conference he was having as a main speaker, but then the conference never came to pass. In fact, he'd never even called attention to the fact that his conference never came to pass, and I'd written him off sometime earlier because of that. He became one of many individuals who did the "I think you are wonderful; we have to have you" song and dance that never materialized. So imagine my surprise when, after a very long period of time, I received an inbox from this same man, consisting of a long-winded prayer for my ministry and my successes. I didn't respond to it much. I said, "thank you" and "amen," and left it at that. Something didn't sit right with me. The next thing I know, there's an event invite in my inbox to attend his preaching event, about seven hours away from me in western Georgia.

I gave much thought and posted a status about the spirit behind the inbox I received from this man, because that same attitude, that same presumptuous spirit, is present in so many people I have dealt with over the years. There have been so many individuals who, for whatever reason, invited me to their conferences or churches and then never followed through on these events...then turned around and expect me to come hear them preach when they are doing something somewhere else. Then there were those who outright told me they were considering me, then told me they didn't feel I was right for the conference but invited me to come to it as a congregant or spectator! There's something about this that just doesn't sit right with me; I think it's the vanity behind it. Instead of working to raise others up and build up the Kingdom, it's obvious our conferences and events have become efforts in trying to create a certain atmosphere or appearance that will launch a leader or ministry to celebrity stardom. As a result, everyone becomes dispensable: it's all about who will bring in the most money or attention, and we can forget about anyone and everyone else who might have something to offer that might bring change.

My status, in summary, stated that while many of us have been associates for some time, some of us have simply not connected. While I acknowledge not everyone is right for everything all the time, that is different from not being considered at all or being considered and then being thrown out. It is unreasonable to suggest I, or anyone in such a position for that matter, should jump across states to events for others when we are not considered worthy to do such. One comment I got on the status was: "Apostle, what God has invested in you is PRICELE$$, and anything that's PRICELE$$ is NOT on clearance. Invest in those that invest in you."

Thanks, I needed that. I'm not on clearance, and I shouldn't live or operate like I am. The gifts of God might come free, but the anointing is priceless. Recognizing the value in the anointing makes all the difference. When we see it for what it is, we will no longer devalue it.

Here's to the reminder that whatever is within you is not

on clearance.

- Day 38 -
When Others Interfere in Your Relationship With God

> HE WILL NOT BE MOVED FOREVER; THE [UNCOMPROMISINGLY] RIGHTEOUS
> (THE UPRIGHT, IN RIGHT STANDING WITH GOD) SHALL BE IN EVERLASTING REMEMBRANCE.
> HE SHALL NOT BE AFRAID OF EVIL TIDINGS; HIS HEART IS FIRMLY FIXED, TRUSTING
> (LEANING ON AND BEING CONFIDENT) IN THE LORD. HIS HEART IS ESTABLISHED
> *AND* STEADY, HE WILL NOT BE AFRAID WHILE HE WAITS TO SEE HIS DESIRE ESTABLISHED
> UPON HIS ADVERSARIES.
> (PSALM 112:6-8)

READING: PROVERBS 3:1-8

IT'S common for us to define our relationship with God as "personal." We like the idea that we have an interaction with God that never runs interference with others, and that it's just us and Him. This is a little simplistic to the reality, however. Our relationship with God is largely shaped by our spiritual influences. The character and nature of God and His voice to us tends to take the form of whatever we are used to hearing. It doesn't mean we are really hearing from God in these instances, but we are definitely shaped in our concept of God and what He sounds like from others. No matter how much we like the idea of a prayer closet or trying to hide ourselves away for Him, if we aren't properly taught how to discern God for ourselves, we will just hear the voices of others when we earnestly seek God.

A few years ago, I was in a situation that left me questioning what I should do, I desired to push myself to do something, anything, so things could get better. It was toward the end of the year and as was customary for me to do, I wanted so much for things to be different, I was just about willing to do anything that would get me away from where I was. At this time, I had an assistant who was very opinionated and very free with his advice. More than once, he had been critical of the thoughts or perspectives I had about things, and he was highly resistant to any suggestions that he might be wrong. He came to me one day with his word, presented it as if it was something I should have already known, and told me it was what I was supposed to be doing. The catch is, I knew it wasn't something I was supposed to do, not by a long shot. When I confronted him about it, I tried to do it nicely, because I didn't want to have a big, long, drawn-out fight that took our whole day away from the task at hand. His response to me was, "I'm not wrong!" That started me on a whole new course of not worrying so much about how much the argument took from my day. This was my life, this was something he was expecting me to do and take care of, and he refused to consider the fact that I hear from God myself and I knew what he was telling me was not really from God. Since I was the one who had to live with the consequences of doing what he was telling me I had to do, I felt like I deserved some sort of say in it. That led to an argument, which led to an enlightenment that might seem kind of obvious: we need to be careful what we say to others, especially when we claim God is in it. Our words don't just have the potential to change someone's life; they have the potential to run interference with what God is saying to them or where He is leading them. What we say, if it is said out of season, turn, or without the Spirit, could seriously alter someone's spiritual course.

I think we sometimes treat giving a "word" as if it's not a serious thing. Whenever we exercise a spiritual gift of any sort, it's a serious undertaking. It's not being done to have a good time or feel good; it's done to convey the word of God and relay His heart in the lives of others. If too much word is impeding your relationship with God, maybe it's time to cut back on the words of others and find some divine guidance, through solid leadership and personal devotion, so you can really hear what God has to say to you right now in your life.

- Day 39 -
Still Hot as Hell

CHARM *AND* GRACE ARE DECEPTIVE, AND BEAUTY IS VAIN [BECAUSE IT IS NOT LASTING],
BUT A WOMAN WHO REVERENTLY *AND* WORSHIPFULLY FEARS THE LORD, SHE SHALL
BE PRAISED!
(PROVERBS 31:30)

READING: 1 SAMUEL 25:1-27

CHRISTIAN women spend a lot of time worrying about their appearance. No matter who we work with, someone always finds something distasteful about our clothing or makeup. There are still groups that judge a woman's salvation by how long or short her skirt is, if she wears makeup, how much makeup she wears, or how long or short her hair is. There are still churches that forbid women to enter the church building without a hat or skirt on, and even churches that take more liberal stances on such things often have unspoken rules that express disapproval about different attire and cosmetic issues among their women.

I tried for many years to adjust myself to the different standards that exist for women, especially when I was a visitor or guest in someone else's church. This wasn't possible, because everyone has different rules. Even with inquiries there were usually unspoken guidelines. There were even a few times when I wore things that were within all the guidelines, but someone still took issue with what I had on, anyway.

When I walked into this season, I still cared. As I walk out of it, I don't care anymore. What changed me was an experience I had as apostle over a traditional Apostolic church back a few years ago. I was involved in the church on a grassroots level, and that meant being directly involved in the weekly teachings and events. We mandated, due to the traditional nature of the church, that I and the other women should wear skirts or dresses in the church as a statement of modeling and appropriateness. At the time, I was in several churches where the women were not dressed appropriately. Seeing too many pants that were too tight, too many bra straps showing in off-the-shoulder tops, and makeup that would have been too bold even for the circus, I was good with the idea. I was good with it until I was having to put on pantyhose three times per week and find dresses for every occasion while the men of the church showed up for Bible study in jeans. I remember looking out over the congregation and saying to myself, "If they can wear jeans, how come I can't wear a pair of pants?"

In that second, caring about what others thought of my clothing ended. Yes, we need to use good judgment, but the Bible encourages us, as women, to avoid such preoccupation with outward adornment that we forget about important things, such as our character. That preoccupation can go two ways. Impressing people with our attire isn't always about trying to show up others by wearing designer labels. Sometimes we are trying to impress others in the church with how good we are at mastering the challenges of church expectations: making sure our clothes fit the rules made by men, and being a mental standard to others for how to polish those rules to perfection.

I'm not 18 anymore, and admittedly, I can't get away with some of what I used to wear back then. Then again, I'm not competing with my former self, or any other woman in the church. The church might not like it, but I'm still hot as hell, not because of the clothes I wear, although dressing to make a statement is something I've always liked to do. I'm hot as hell because integrity makes me strong, and strong women will be attractive no matter what they wear. In other words:

I'll wear what I want, I'll show up and show out, and whoever doesn't like it...just doesn't matter.

- DAY 40 -
Becoming Neo-Apostolic

DO NOT [EARNESTLY] REMEMBER THE FORMER THINGS; NEITHER CONSIDER THE THINGS
OF OLD. BEHOLD, I AM DOING A NEW THING! NOW IT SPRINGS FORTH; DO YOU NOT PERCEIVE
AND KNOW IT *AND* WILL YOU NOT GIVE HEED TO IT? I WILL EVEN MAKE A WAY
IN THE WILDERNESS AND RIVERS IN THE DESERT.
(ISAIAH 43:18-19)

READING: EZEKIEL 36:24-32

WHEN I started Apostolic Fellowship International Ministries in 2004, I named the ministry in accord with the traditional understanding of what it meant to be "apostolic." For a few generations, the term "apostolic" was associated exclusively with an ultra-traditional Pentecostal affiliate that held to extreme views on many social and theological matters, such as women and men's attire, speaking in tongues in relation to salvation, baptism in relation to salvation, and end times peripherals. The groups that identified themselves as "apostolic" have always been more on the fringes of spiritual acceptance and many Christian denominations shun them. At the time, however, I was one, albeit a bad one. I believed in the faith and practice of the apostles as applicable for today and I had received baptism in Jesus' Name, but that was about the very moment where my attempts at being a good, denominational apostolic ended. I have hair that must be cut, or it looks like a rat's nest. Where I lived in New York State meant pants equaled warm legs in the dead of winter. Wearing a skirt everywhere was largely impractical, and the many other rules and regulations apostolics had didn't generally fit with who I was. I tried, and I did my best, despite the fact that my efforts were simply not good enough.

Over time, "apostolic" became more than a denomination; it became a marker of believing in the five-fold ministry and the relevance of apostles, so our ministry identity became associated more with that than an apostolic denomination. I was perfectly content with this, and my new-found freedom, until God gave me the term "neo-Apostolic" about nine years ago. At the time, I didn't know what it meant. I thought being apostolic in a five-fold sense was good enough and understandable enough for the work done in the ministry, and I never considered a viable change. I had no idea "neo-Apostolic" would ever become a thing or mean anything, except maybe an ideology I'd embrace for myself.

Just last week, my spiritual daughter came to me with the question of what her spiritual identity was, because she wasn't sure anymore. Through a long conversation, I came out saying that we are "neo-Apostolic." The term literally means "new apostolic." In other words, we are apostolic for a new era. We are five-fold, we embrace and respect the traditions of believers past, we believe in properly understanding the idea of holiness in a genuine context, we believe in understanding the doctrine of the apostles for today, we respect our history, and above all, we believe in the need to make faith applicable and practical for our modern era. This means preaching and teaching needs to relate to now, not the things we hold onto as believers that usually don't apply much for right now. We're about letting go, letting God fill us with His Spirit, and letting that Spirit work within us in ways we cannot work ourselves. We are about now. We are about being apostolic, in its truest definition, right now: we are about changing the world, just like the first believers did in those first decades of Christianity.

It's not hard to embrace now, but considering where I was thirteen years ago, I never would have imagined God wanted to use this work to do something new. Through tradition, through change, through progress, and through understanding, I have become something new. It didn't just come through initial conversion; it came as I lived my faith, walking it out day in and day out with diligence.

- Day 41 -
Coming to the End of Myself

HE MUST INCREASE, BUT I MUST DECREASE. [HE MUST GROW MORE PROMINENT;
I MUST GROW LESS SO.]
(JOHN 3:30)

Reading: Mark 8:34-38

IF I were to summarize the overall theme of my current season, I would define it as "coming to the end of myself." This might sound like an odd thing for a minister to say, but the truth of every minister is we are all very human. Sometimes our own hang-ups lurk just beneath the surface, and we don't know they are there until they are challenged. Many of these issues, be they our own unique prejudices, traditions, ideals, or concepts all gather together and form our concepts of Christian life and ministry to the exclusion of spiritual understanding. If we allow ourselves to go down this road, our ministries become an extension of our concepts and those of others instead of what God desires them to be.

When we talk about the Spirit working through us (as we often do), I don't think we have the first clue of what we are talking about if we haven't experienced it. The whole concept of being Spirit-filled means we are so full of the presence of God within us, there is no longer room for us, as ourselves, to get in the way of that. There are too many times where we know what will rile others in the flesh and instead of making the way for that spiritual experience we know God desires, we pursue and speak in the flesh, making that appear to be something deep or spiritual.

It wasn't that I was a total washout or self-centered

person prior to this experience. Quite the contrary, in fact. Much of my thought life compared myself to others and what I was doing wrong, because others seemed more effective in ministry than I was. Yet the reality remained that the shape of my ministry resembled that of everyone else's way too much. I adopted a posture, a form, and a style that was like everything else that was out there. By watching what was around me, I'd become the minister I thought I should be, and the type of minister I defined, rather than allowing God to take over and work through me in a deep and powerful way.

He had to increase, and I had to decrease. It wasn't anything like we often speak of it in reality; it was something else entirely. Allowing God to increase meant I had to come to the end of every concept, idea, and thought process I had about who I was to minister to and how I was supposed to do it.

Being in ministry is about more than just loving God and saying we love people (although these are fine concepts). It's about allowing God to work within us so that we become living love; that walking, living, breathing impression of the way God loves us. It might be cute to preach down a house while wearing the best outfit in the room but doing that doesn't transform or change anyone. Years and years of this proves it doesn't work, especially as we all go on with our regular lives and avoid the uncomfortable questions and discussions that address just how far away from our faith we've become. Such things are entertaining, but not always fulfilling of purpose. To be a minister God could use, I had to come to an end of myself. I had to release myself from all those people, ideals, and things that had become idols in my life and hindered the flow of God from working in and through me.

My experience as He increased and I decreased changed everything about me as a minister, but in a deeper sense, it changed me as a person. I saw myself in a light I never had before: emptied, ready to be filled, finding no place so overwhelmed and full it could not be drenched, saturated, and imparted with His Spirit.

- Day 42 -
Putting on the Shoes of Peace

STAND THEREFORE [HOLD YOUR GROUND], HAVING TIGHTENED THE BELT OF TRUTH
AROUND YOUR LOINS AND HAVING PUT ON THE BREASTPLATE OF INTEGRITY *AND* OF
MORAL RECTITUDE *AND* RIGHT STANDING WITH GOD, AND HAVING SHOD YOUR FEET
IN PREPARATION [TO FACE THE ENEMY WITH THE FIRM-FOOTED STABILITY,
THE PROMPTNESS, AND THE READINESS PRODUCED BY THE GOOD NEWS]
OF THE GOSPEL OF PEACE.
(EPHESIANS 6:14-15)

READING: ROMANS 14:16-19

I have a confession: My name is Lee Ann, and I am a shoeaholic. Granted such a thing is not real, or at least it is not real in a clinical sense, anyone who knows me knows I love my shoes. I first got interested in shoes because I noticed I was much more comfortable standing and preaching in heels than in flats or other types of footwear. This is due to an abnormally high arch and supination, a condition where my feet turn out on their sides instead of sustaining flat. Sneakers and flats are often uncomfortable. Standing in them for long periods of time just doesn't work. When I discovered heels did work, I decided to run with it. I was also a little more of a subdued dresser in my past, so shoes became a form of self-expression, a way to dress up and make a statement without being too overdone. It's gone from a practical expression to an all-out hobby, and so notable some people follow me on social media, just to see what shoes I wear when going out!

Yes, I love shoes, I love wearing them, photographing them, and collecting them, but for the past few years, I have been learning to embrace a different kind of shoe: the shoes of peace. The Scriptures talk about the shoes of the "Gospel of peace" in Ephesians as part of spiritual armor for believers. It's easy to breeze past the expression and not think much of it, especially in light of other pieces of armor that sound more intense or explorative. Yet any good shoe connoisseur will tell you the shoes make the outfit; thus the shoes of peace make or break our spiritual armor. The more I go along, the more I find this to be true.

I am a self-admitted hothead. I get impatient when people don't understand and equally frustrated when people don't listen or don't receive what is said. I'm not alone in this; the Apostle Peter was a bit of a hothead himself. Even the Apostle Paul himself sounded a bit temperamental in some of his letters. Yes, we can get angry over spiritual things and we can even be angry for the right reasons, but lashing out in anger often takes on a fleshly character. We can be angry just for the sake of being angry sometimes, especially if we are honest with ourselves. Calming our anger, tempering our tempers, and learning to handle our emotions in a constructive way goes a long way in applying the Gospel to ourselves personally, in an up-close way that is sometimes uncomfortable, but important, in the long run.

Peace is spoken of in terms of footwear for one simple reason: it is something we put on last and gives us the ability to tread properly on the terrain we encounter nowadays. It's something we must put on, something we must deliberately endeavor to explore as we are honest with ourselves and our temperaments. Peace doesn't come for many of us naturally. It takes a unique person to look over life and the complications it often bears with a sense of peace. I know for myself, it is a deliberate action, something I must think about, just as I have to think about what shoes go with what outfit and whether they match or make the desired statement. Peace only goes with our outfit of spiritual armor if we deliberately put it on, make it apply, and bring the rest of ourselves into conformity with where our peaceful feet seek to go.

I've never had daisies spring up as I walk in peace, but I can say with assurance, I've had some better situations as a result. Not to mention, a far better witness that reaches far more people. The right shoes can make any situation right.

- Day 43 -
A Little Bit Christian, A Little Bit Rock and Roll

Do not be conformed to this world (this age), [fashioned after and adapted to its external, superficial customs], but be transformed (changed) by the [entire] renewal of your mind [by its new ideals and its new attitude], so that you may prove [for yourselves] what is the good and acceptable and perfect will of God, *even* the thing which is good and acceptable and perfect [in His sight for you].
(Romans 12:2)

Reading: Galatians 1:1-12

IF I were to describe myself to someone else, I'd probably have a hard time. I don't think it's ever easy for us to explain ourselves and our nature to others, especially given we don't perceive ourselves the same way that others do. I often make the joke that no matter how good you might tell a woman that she looks, she still thinks she's a cow. The same is true with any specific perspectives we might have about ourselves. Someone else might consider me a technical genius, but I think I'm all right at what I do. Someone else might laud the ministry, and I might not think it's where I want it to be. Still, there are those who might have something contrary to say, something that questions the work or integrity of the ministry for one major reason: I am different.

It's taken me many years to admit that, as I am sure you can gather from the devotions of past days. I tried to fit in, but I didn't. In fact, I have never fit in, 100%, anywhere I have been. I've done better in some places than others, but the truth is that I have never entirely conformed anywhere. One of my friends calls me a "non-conformist," and I love it. The reason for this is simple: I don't feel that any place has all the answers. Some might think so, but if the only way for me to fit in is to resemble all your rules, then that tells me something about your rules: they are made by men.

Traditions are funny things. They leave us complacent and comfortable, but we are quick to pick them up when the systems we follow fail us in some way. They help us maintain our identities as whatever we are, especially when we know whatever it is just isn't working or has questions within it. They keep us a lot Christian, and avoid anything that makes us a little bit rock and roll. Tradition makes the two opposites; it makes it so that we can't be anything but...well...steeped in traditional ideals and roles.

I've spent years experiencing tradition and have been on both sides of the traditional debate. I've been steeped in tradition, lived in tradition, and tried to fit my non-conforming self into the traditional mold. Still, there's always been a part of me that remains a little bit rock and roll. I like leather dress suits, I am not real demure, and...well...tradition has this nasty way of boring me. I like energy and excitement, and I never want to be so untouchable and unapproachable because I can't relate to issues in the real world. If it's possible to combine the energy of rock star with the energy of Christian, I'd like to think I meet with the definition.

None of us should get so lost in fitting in, conforming to an abstract version of belief manifest through the rules of men that we lose touch with the things going on in this world and being people who are likable and pleasant. I've said for years that starting off a conversation with "where will you spend eternity?" is a lousy way to get a conversation started. If we are so traditional that we've lost sight of life, enjoying life and being able to relate to people, we've lost sight of the whole purpose in belief. We need to be Christian enough to transform and real enough to bring life and hope to situations that lack the essence of life.

So don't be surprised if you see me in my typical non-conforming style, talking with someone about rock and roll, jeans, fashion, or television. It's all part of the process; nothing binds me, nor hinders. I am sowing seeds for life, so people know where to come when they are ready for whatever's next.

- Day 44 -
Inspired Busyness

> So I saw that there is nothing better than that a man should rejoice
> in his own works, for that is his portion. For who shall bring him back
> to see what will happen after he is gone?
> (Ecclesiastes 3:22)

Reading: John 5:13-20

WHEN I approached the end of my season, I was filled with a profound sense of...nothing. The months leading up to its end were insanely quiet, save for the occasional interpersonal crisis someone was having on any given day. It was probably not an abnormal or unusual thing; it was just a...boring thing. I've spent many years of my life busy and active, so not having a lot to do felt wrong. It also left me feeling uninspired.

Don't get me wrong, I acknowledge that being busy just to be busy isn't a good thing. I have spent time in my life doing that, too, and it led to literal exhaustion without much purpose. There was a time in my life when I was just busy being busy, because it made me feel important or indispensable, or something equally stupid as that, and it wasted a lot of time. But I am a person who finds true inspiration in doing things and being busy. So, when things are slow, and not moving much, I don't have the problem of busy distractions, I have the problem of lackluster boredom.

I had been working on two books: one from the end of last year and this one, which I started early in the year. The process for both went relatively well, until things slowed down so much, I started to lose interest in writing them. This hadn't happened to me in a good long while, since before I started publishing. Given I write most days, sometimes all day, it felt strange. I just didn't want to write. I wanted to spend the time doing something else: binge watching a television show, sewing, maybe reading, anything but spending extensive time trying to write. The pages seemed blank, the words were few and far between, and I had no idea, mind you no idea, what I wanted to say when I wanted to say it.

That was until I picked up a new publishing job. It wasn't even a full-scale job! I was assisting a self-published author with some layout and cover design for existing books he wanted to gravitate over to a new publishing forum. It had been a few months since I had a current client, and I was grateful for the work. Sometimes completing older contracts gets tedious and having someone new to work for and with was a good experience for me. As I sat and looked over his text, laid out his book and designed a cover, I was suddenly flooded with different ideas for my own book. I wasn't drawing on his writing, which was quite different from my own. There was just something about being busy and having something to do, doing something for someone else and doing something for work, that gave me ideas and purpose for my own work. I went from not wanting to touch it with a pole to being so into it, I stayed up half the night to work on things!

Sometimes we assume the answer to inspiration is found in rest or ceasing to work instead of connecting ourselves to something we love doing and drawing inspiration from it. Yes, rest is sometimes necessary, but when I look at the massive amount of time people spend on fasts, vacations, and "away" from the normal work, it doesn't surprise me when they don't do much else. If we think the answer for inspiration will be found in nothing, we will find ourselves sadly mistaken. Inspiration is all around us: it comes from life, living, and work. If you find yourself uninspired, maybe it's what you are doing, or not doing. Sometimes the best way to jump start into what's next is to get busy doing something you love right now.

- Day 45 -
Fixing the Broken Nail

BUT THEN I WILL BRING HEALTH [RECOVERY] AND HEALING TO THE PEOPLE THERE.
I WILL HEAL THEM AND LET THEM ENJOY [REVEAL TO THEM] GREAT [AN ABUNDANCE OF] PEACE
AND SAFETY [SECURITY].
(JEREMIAH 33:6, EXB)

READING: DEUTERONOMY 7:11-15

To answer one of the great mysteries about me: yes, my nails are real. They are not acrylic. I seldom wear tips because my fingers are too small, and they pop off too easily. My nails are really my nails and have been since I stopped biting them as a teenager. I'll polish them or do things to dress them up, but I have come to find that I prefer wearing my own natural nails, including growing them out. This takes patience in many instances when they break, because I must wait for them to grow back in.

Of course, this is exactly what just happened last night: my nail broke.

A few weeks ago, I went with my mom to retrieve something of hers from storage. We found a slight mess upon entry, although it was not nearly as bad as I expected it to be. It still involved moving boxes and lifting heavy objects. I was pleased as I could be that none of my nails were ripped off in the process, especially given I had just smacked one of them as hard as imaginable on the bathroom counter the night before. It didn't break then, so I was ready to defend these nails come hell or high water against the boxes in the storage unit. I was so busy being glad my nails didn't obviously break that I failed to notice a small tear a little way down one of my nails that bent during the unpacking and repacking process.

I made it a little over two weeks with it staying on. It was a total nuisance in the meantime. I tried gluing it, filing it, tucking it behind the existing base nail, but it wouldn't stay. It snagged on literally everything and got caught on towels, embroidery floss, jeans, shirts, and cotton pants. Every time it got stuck, it pulled a little more and stuck out just that much further to make sure everything else would catch it, too.

I had no choice but to rip it off to make sure it wouldn't tear all the way down where it had cracked. Cutting it wasn't an option, because the tear was too low, and I had no choice but to suck up the moment and rip my nail off. As I did it, I looked at the former glory that my nail had been, and something came to me.

We like to be people who fix things instead of letting things follow their own course, healing, and starting over again. We'll do all the things to our situations that I tried to do to my nail: we'll try to mend things somehow, or avoid catching the situation off guard, or we'll try to cut it or otherwise rectify it in a way that will salvage it where it is, but those approaches often don't work. Sometimes the only answer for a situation is to literally rip it off, let what remains heal or grow back into something else, and start all over again.

That's why we don't want to do it: we don't want to start all over again. I certainly didn't with my nail. It had taken me months to get them to their length, solid and healthy looking, and the idea of having to wait out more time while this one nail grew back in wasn't appealing. Yet after I ripped the nail off, filed down what remained and evened it out, the prospect of having to wait out its regrowth wasn't that scary anymore. It was what it was, it would return as it always does, and there was no reason at all to spend more time giving it another thought. My nail broke, as nails often do. Trying to live around my broken nail had become a job in and of itself, and I was tired of doing that. It will be back soon enough, as will our lives, if we only let our situations rip off, standoff, grow back, and then ultimately, heal.

- Day 46 -
Divine Hints

SAMUEL SAID, HAS THE LORD AS GREAT A DELIGHT IN BURNT OFFERINGS AND SACRIFICES AS IN OBEYING THE VOICE OF THE LORD? BEHOLD, TO OBEY IS BETTER THAN SACRIFICE, AND TO HEARKEN THAN THE FAT OF RAMS. FOR REBELLION IS AS THE SIN OF WITCHCRAFT, AND STUBBORNNESS IS AS IDOLATRY AND TERAPHIM (HOUSEHOLD GOOD LUCK IMAGES). BECAUSE YOU HAVE REJECTED THE WORD OF THE LORD, HE ALSO HAS REJECTED YOU FROM BEING KING.
(1 SAMUEL 15:22-23)

READING: EPHESIANS 2:1-10

ONE night I was in the car with someone who wanted to stop by the ATM in order to get some cash for a purchase. The purchase wasn't thousands of dollars, but it was in the hundreds. (As far as I am concerned, it was a pretty sizeable expense.) When at the first (yes, I said first) ATM, there was a sign that said it was out of service. While on the way to the second ATM, he told me, "If this one is out of order, I am going to take that as a sign from God to just be on my way and forget this." Sure enough, we drive up to the second ATM, and it's out of service. Instead of humbly accepting it as a sign received, he was on to a third ATM, complete with grumbling, hostility, and complaining the whole way. The third ATM was working, and the money was withdrawn. Still, the question remains: what about the promise, that came out of the individual's mouth, that they would take it as a sign from God that they shouldn't make this purchase?

The answer is easy and complicated, both at the same time. Yes, he certainly received a "divine hint" that came from the Lord; it came straight from their own mouth. The item in question was desired; it was desired more than obedience. That might be an ouch moment, but it's true, nonetheless. Signs or not, the person in question wanted the item more than they wanted to obey God. There was no consideration for patience or waiting, or maybe even that the item wasn't necessary or wasn't right for that moment. Whatever the reason might have been, it was a case of wanting something more than wanting whatever God desired.

We don't like to consider our relationship with God as a personalized battle ground, but in many ways, it is. Throughout our lives, we war between the flesh and the Spirit, between what we want and what we don't want to surrender. Whether it's as simple as not buying something or disciplining ourselves for greater things (by studying or behaving better), we don't easily yield to God's hints, do we? We like to say things like the individual in question said because they sound deep and profound, but when we get those hints, we don't want to take heed of them. We still want what we want, when we want it, and we will use any and all justifications to try and make sure we ignore God's divine hints and do things the way we wanted to in the first place.

We experience divine hints because God doesn't force us to do anything. It is God's will that we will learn the gentle leading of His voice, of the way in which He guides us by the Holy Spirit into all truth. God treats us with respect, giving us the ability to make our own choices, just as parents do with children. We learn to trust His guidance by realizing He knows things we do not know about situations and embrace the principle that He really does want the best for us.

Yes, God does want the best for us. It may not always feel like it, but it is true. This is where trust comes in, and where denial of our flesh plays heavily on our walk with God. Denying our flesh isn't all about avoiding illicit sex and inappropriate clothing, although those are things that we could talk about on another day. Denying our flesh is about saying no to ourselves, to anything that causes us to turn on God or bring our relationship with Him into reproach. If we can't do it with little things, we can't expect big things to bless us in the long run.

- Day 47 -
Snap out of it!

CAN YOUR HEART *AND* COURAGE ENDURE OR CAN YOUR HANDS BE STRONG
IN THE DAYS THAT I SHALL DEAL WITH YOU? I THE LORD HAVE SPOKEN IT, AND I WILL DO IT.
(EZEKIEL 22:14)

READING: PHILIPPIANS 3:7-16

WHO remembers the movie *Moonstruck*, starring Cher and Nicholas Cage? There were many reasons why I loved the movie, and why I still watch it every time they play it again on cable. The first reason, obviously, is because the main characters were all Italian. Long before *Jersey Shore* ruined the image of Italian-Americans on television, the lore of Italian culture found its image in more urban settings, usually New York City. The men are typified as Mafioso or thugs and the women as hard-working, with the power to transform the world with their cooking. *Moonstruck* is no different; it is a movie about love and relationships, how we often find the one "for us" when we aren't looking for it. It's a great story with a message that hits home at all of us, especially when Cher slaps Nicholas Cage across the face and tells him, "Snap out of it!"

Moonstruck always makes me think about many of the deeper questions in life that got answered in a big way for me over the past couple of years. When I sought an answer, I usually found it when I decided to "snap out of it!" and back into reality. Much of what we hold onto revolves around concepts and ideals that we love (be they romantic or not) and we are unwilling to let them go because letting them go means letting go of the fantasies that surround them. That was an underlying theme in *Moonstruck*: the main characters were living what they thought they were supposed to be doing, day in and day out, without any thought to whether it was something that worked for them. In the face of everything to the contrary, they fought what they knew they were supposed to do to hang on for dear life to the concepts and ideals that held them in place and identified their sense of self.

In this season, I have been forced to "snap out of it!" in more than one way. Some of these circumstances, situations, and people have been a big slap in the face to wake up, pay attention, and put aside the romantic notions I held dear that I didn't even know I had. I just assumed I was living life, following a specific course of action, in and out, every day. I didn't realize I had ideals that were unrealistic or involved fantasies, such as concepts about ministry as easy and preaching as a constant spiritual "rush." I thought ministry would just fall into place, and the rest would come from there. I always acknowledged ministry would be some level of work, but not the work I thought it would be. Here and there, all through this season, I got smacked in the face by the realities that plague the work of ministry and the true level of hard endurance it requires to do ministry in the way we must to be effective.

What do you need to "snap out of it" in order to move forward and get the full effect of reality in your life? If we want to be people who make an impact now, in this day and time, we have to live in right now and snap out of the things that keep us bound and hold us tightly, because we don't want to let go. We're quick to talk about the hold of drugs and alcohol or other forms of addiction, but we don't step back and realize some of us are addicted to our ideas, our principles that don't apply or help anyone anymore, or to the ideals that we think will turn our world around and come true if we wish hard enough. They aren't coming to pass; they are just holding us back, and complicating our lives, making sure we won't find what truly awaits us in reality.

- Day 48 -
White and Nerdy

MEDITATE UPON THESE THINGS; GIVE THYSELF WHOLLY TO THEM; THAT THY PROFITING
MAY APPEAR TO ALL. TAKE HEED UNTO THYSELF, AND UNTO THE DOCTRINE;
CONTINUE IN THEM: FOR IN DOING THIS THOU SHALT BOTH SAVE THYSELF, AND THEM
THAT HEAR THEE.
(1 TIMOTHY 4:15-16, KJV)

READING: 1 PETER 3:15-22

TWO days ago someone told me I was a "technical genius." I think this is a bit of a stretch, especially since I feel totally inept when texting on my cell phone. I am a slow…slow…slow texter because texting didn't become a thing until I was in my late twenties. I know that's probably not an excuse, but I wasn't much for it in the beginning, and I've never picked it up. I do still prefer a desktop, which makes it easier for me to see for layout and other technical work. But, in the long run, I guess I see why I have gotten the label as a bit of a nerd. I am a bit of a techie; I like things that have batteries and modems and make noise when I click on something too many times. I learned computers, layout, audio editing, and web design all on my own, without ever taking an official computer class. I grew up in an in-between time when tech was starting to take over but hadn't reached our classrooms in the way it did later in time. Because personal computers were a new thing and finally becoming financially affordable to the average person, most of us took an interest in them, and I was no different. There are some things I can't do, but when it comes down to it, I know enough to be my own moderate tech support and do many technical things on my own.

My nerdy approach to life doesn't just apply to tech. I am also a bit of a nerd when it comes to ministry. Over the past several years, I have dedicated myself to studying various concepts that we talk about and teach in church on a very technical and specific level. It's not an easy undertaking, not by a long shot. It has meant I have to apply myself to minute details and concepts and pay special attention to inconsistencies that exist. The reason I have set myself to do this is simple: there are many, many things we say over and over again in church that have become so commonplace, many of us automatically assume they are facts. We assume it's true that apostles exist to "set order" or that the five-fold ministry is some sort of strange hand diagram. We think prophets are all about houses, money, cars, and various promises that often don't come to pass. We quote Bible verses out of context and do so in such a way we assume our incorrect usage of them is, indeed, the proper way to cite them. The world of Christianity has taken on such a character of personality-driven energy, we have completely abandoned true Biblical understanding, the Spirit of Christ at work in our lives, and proper understanding of truth to chase energetic preachers.

Someone has got to dedicate themselves to understanding spiritual things beyond the fun personalities that often demand and command our attention, at the same time. Yes, praising God should be something we enjoy, but there is also a time to learn and focus our energies on things other than our own personal entertainment. If the only reason we go to church is to run around, sing songs we know by heart, and receive constant encouragement without correction, we are missing the whole point and purpose in going to church. Someone, somewhere must make the time to be technical, to be nerdy, to discipline us and teach us where we are, right now, today.

Someone must do it. Might as well be me. It's not like I

have anything better to do with my life.

- Day 49 -
Identification

BUT WE ARE CITIZENS OF THE STATE (COMMONWEALTH, HOMELAND) WHICH IS IN HEAVEN, AND FROM IT ALSO WE EARNESTLY *AND* PATIENTLY AWAIT [THE COMING OF] THE LORD JESUS CHRIST (THE MESSIAH) [AS] SAVIOR, WHO WILL TRANSFORM *AND* FASHION ANEW THE BODY OF OUR HUMILIATION TO CONFORM TO *AND* BE LIKE THE BODY OF HIS GLORY *AND* MAJESTY, BY EXERTING THAT POWER WHICH ENABLES HIM EVEN TO SUBJECT EVERYTHING TO HIMSELF.
(PHILIPPIANS 3:20-21)

READING: 1 CORINTHIANS 12:12-27

I am a natural redhead. Not a Little Orphan Annie color redhead or a Lucy Ball (which was not real) redhead, but a dark, nasty-color red that didn't go with my complexion. Nobody else had my hair color. Nobody else wanted my hair color. Adults told me how lucky I was to have it. As far as I was concerned, they could all have it if they thought it was so wonderful. Nobody had it. Nobody looked like me. Nobody in my immediate or extended family had the same color. When you are a kid, all you want to do is see someone who looks like you, so you don't feel so different.

I remembered back a few weeks ago about how long and hard I looked when I was a kid to identify with someone, someone who looked like me. I was searching for redheads. Next to no one had red hair. I found Danny Bonaduce on the *Partridge Family* and Ariel in *The Little Mermaid*. Nobody else had red hair, and neither one had hair close to my color. Danny Bonaduce won over Ariel because not only was he redheaded, he was also Italian, which was the closest I ever got to seeing a reflection of myself on television. Still, I wanted to identify. I wanted to see something on television or in the movies that reflected what I saw in myself when I looked in the mirror.

Identification is something many professionals speak of as a vital aspect of belonging and healthy self-image within society. It's all a gigantic code for "we all want to belong" somewhere and to feel like we fit in with other people. It's something we strive for in a world that is different, full of different people and different ideals. We like to be comfortable; if we are the redhead, we like to meet the other redhead; if we are somehow different, we like to meet the people who are the same kind of different as we are.

I decided recently that being a Christian is an identification process. It's not any different from me growing up, hoping I would see a redhead on TV. Being a Christian is about becoming a new creature in Christ. In the process, we must reorient ourselves to something different than we are used to. It doesn't mean we are suddenly something other than we are as long as we are in this body. We're still our nations of origin. We probably look the same and sound the same, and we speak the same language and hand employers the same birth certificate. Yet there is supposed to be something different about us, a change that creates a difference in us. No longer is our identity solely of this world but is now about being a part of the strive as citizens of heaven. We aren't just supposed to want to find people who look like us; we are supposed to unite to others who believe in Christ as we do and pursue the work of the Kingdom with them.

Identity in the sense of this world has caused a lot of problems throughout history. It's led to both feelings of inferiority for those who don't find identification with others and feelings of superiority when groups of people decided to lord certain attributes above those others had. In Christ, our identifying hostilities are to cease in favor of something more important: eternity. If we will only put on the nature of Christ, cease our hostilities and see ourselves in the light of spiritual eyes, as children of God, rather than children of this world.

- Day 50 -
Good Stewardship

As each of you has received a gift (a particular spiritual talent, a gracious divine endowment), employ it for one another as [befits] good trustees of God's many-sided grace [faithful stewards of the extremely diverse powers and gifts granted to Christians by unmerited favor].
(1 Peter 4:10)

Reading: Luke 12:42-46

STEWARDSHIP is a fancy word for "management." When we talk about good stewardship, we are referring to a principle of being able to manage different aspects of our lives and personal being well. Good stewardship isn't just about how we handle our money or perform on our jobs, although it certainly does apply in those instances, too. Good stewardship is a foundational attitude by which we govern ourselves and everything that impacts us, from our emotions and our spiritual states to our actions and personal conducts.

I never gave much thought to stewardship before this season reared its complicated and often challenging head. Stewardship was one of those things we didn't consider that often, so we never studied it. Yet when I started to look around and see the different issues present in the church today, I realized much of what we deal with relates to poor stewardship. If we pay more attention to what we are doing and how we do it, things might be different.

When I started this season, we had a reasonable amount of money coming into the ministry. It wasn't a million dollars, but it was certainly better than it had been in years past, and it was more than many ministers I knew had as monthly profit. I was satisfied with where we were, at least for the most part. I adjusted to the income we had coming in, was comfortable handling the money, and to the income and outgoing we had. There wasn't much more to it than that until one by one, my major financial backers all backed out. Their reasons varied, but within a period of less than three weeks, I lost all three of the major financers this ministry had. It was shocking, to say the least, but also a scary time. How was the ministry going to make it? I knew my life had changes coming, as well, so how in the world was I going to be able to sustain myself with such a huge backward step?

The answer was through good stewardship. Just as I had easily adjusted to the amount of money we had coming in, I also adjusted to the amount of money I now didn't have. I had to learn about buying in online auctions and applying the knowledge I had to different situations that pertained to stewardship. I also had to adjust my feelings about things to a precept of good stewardship. Every time I went and looked at the bank account and was face-to-face with reality, I would get angry all over again. Our lack of finances and the requirement to be a good steward with them made me aware of all sorts of things connected to life and spending: buying out of emotion, questioning whether or not something is really needed, handling emotions and not comparing our situation to someone else, cleaning up aspects of my business that would make me a better independent contractor, and just becoming a person who wasn't so easily pulled by the different strings people often try to use to control through finances. It was about being a better steward, a more competent servant who can serve, regardless of both financial limitations and exterior circumstances.

Good stewardship isn't a perfect science. There are many angles and aspects to it that cause us to shift, examine, and change, all over again. Some nights it's hard, some days it's uncomfortable. Waiting to do things until the time is right is crucial, and often raises impatience. If we want to move from where we are into something else, however, it is undeniably necessary.

- Day 51 -
I'm not Short, I'm Ultra-Concentrated Awesome

I WILL CONFESS *AND* PRAISE YOU *FOR YOU ARE FEARFUL AND WONDERFUL
AND* FOR THE AWFUL WONDER OF MY BIRTH! WONDERFUL ARE YOUR WORKS,
AND THAT MY INNER SELF KNOWS RIGHT WELL.
(PSALM 139:14)

READING: GENESIS 1:26-31

WHENEVER I get an inbox asking about my height, people are shocked to find out that I am 4'11." Yes. I'm short. I am not tall. I am never going to be tall. The messages go from shock and astonishment to protests. "No way! I figured you were at least 5'10!" "Um, no. Never going to be 5'10." Not even in a pair of six-inch stilettos. It's just not in my cards. This is my height. I accept it. It is what it is, even if I cried when they told me I was done growing when I was about 13. I'm not tall enough to be a model. I'm built in accordance with my Italian ancestry, which means I look like someone concentrated a whole lot of me into a very small package. My words don't lie. This is, literally...me.

Being short has its downsides. One of the biggest ones for me, personally, is my interest in fashion. Things are not typically tailored when they are mass-produced, and this means garments are made with specific dimensions in mind. When you're short, it's not just your legs that don't measure up to make an incredible height. I've got small hands, small feet, short legs and a short torso, which all measure up to make clothing difficult to find and fit just right. I stopped buying off the rack several years ago when measurements and sizing changed to what's now known as "vanity sizing."

Vanity sizing changed the way women's clothes fit, and it has also screwed with our sense of sizing. What this equates with is simple: sizes now vary by style and brand, and it's possible to wear three or four different sizes depending on where you shop and what you are looking for. If you always wore a size 10, you might now be an 8, a 12, or a 14, depending on who makes that garment. This is all frustrating enough, so now consider the height and size in the factor. Sometimes patterns on a garment are too large for my size, sometimes things that fit otherwise fine are just too long, and even petite sizes must be hemmed. I love fashion and I take an interest in style and design, but also accept some styles and designs are hard for me to wear (or don't fit properly).

I never, ever used to take my height into consideration when buying clothes. I would buy things, thinking no matter what they looked like, it would be all right in the long run. The result were many designs that looked matronly, made me look 20 years older than I am, and some things just didn't look like they fit very well. Going through my closet, deciding what to give away and what to keep, has been a most interesting adventure, as I examine not just color or what looks good on a hanger, but what really looks good on me.

We should all be willing to take the time to embrace the idea that we are unique and what makes us unique is more than just a personality quirk or concept of ourselves that we show to the world. The Scriptures teach us that we are fearfully and wonderfully made. Yes, it's not easy to stand out from a standard mold set for us by society, but there's something so ominous about society's way of making us feel inferior, because we aren't someone else. I've found ways around my height with buying. I must be more careful with what I wear and pay close attention to what looks good on me. I can't say I know what it's like to see the top of people's heads or slam-dunk a basketball. I do know what it's like to walk under things people run into and fit into spaces most can't squeeze. No, I don't know what it's like to be tall and stun everyone in the room...but I can wear really cool shoes that others can't.

- Day 52 -
His Heart Trusts in Her

A CAPABLE, INTELLIGENT, *AND* VIRTUOUS WOMAN—WHO IS HE WHO CAN FIND HER?
SHE IS FAR MORE PRECIOUS THAN JEWELS *AND* HER VALUE IS FAR ABOVE RUBIES *OR* PEARLS.
THE HEART OF HER HUSBAND TRUSTS IN HER CONFIDENTLY *AND* RELIES ON AND BELIEVES
IN HER SECURELY, SO THAT HE HAS NO LACK OF [HONEST] GAIN OR NEED OF [DISHONEST]
SPOIL.
(PROVERBS 31:10-11)

READING: 1 PETER 3:3-4

I'VE only heard a few teachings in the past few years; I have just heard the same ones, over and over again, by different people. If they aren't talking about money, they are talking about success. If they aren't talking about strange concepts that aren't Biblical as pertain to the apostolic, they are talking about witchcraft. If it's not witchcraft, it's Jezebel. If it's not politics, it's marriage. I have heard the good, bad, and the indifferent on marriage, but I would hesitate to say I haven't found many teachings on marriage that I am willing to endorse.

I fully well admit that marriage is a tricky topic for teaching. It echoes of our own relationship issues and regrets. What I most often see are marital theories put forth as truth, based in one's personal lamentations of what they didn't do right in their intimate relationships and what they would like to have done differently. Their laments aren't typically Biblical, although they might conveniently stretch a few Bible passages to make it fit. Most of the advice I see follows typical Americana form on relationships: women are in tow and men are in control, and if everyone would just fit into the nice

American ideal of household-ism, everything would be fine.

This oversimplification of relationships is most disheartening to me, let alone discouraging. I have never met a married couple that ever fell into a singular category or role. We're not roles, we are people, and marriage is a complicated mix of gifts and callings that come together somehow, some way, hopefully with a good outcome. It's not always easy and it's not always simple, and trying to define modern relationships based on Biblical systems that no longer exist isn't always the easiest way to understand them. Yet in the middle of the Bible, in Proverbs 31 nonetheless, we find an interesting injunction that we never hear in Biblical teaching about marriage and relationships: his heart trusts in her. For a marriage to work, spouses must trust in each other.

It hasn't been my experience to be in an intimate relationship where I would say someone's heart "trusted in me." Maybe one day, but to this point, I have lived with and experienced the intense struggles and difficulties created by bad advice and old-world values that never worked. It's a part of our culture, a result of the fact that in our relationships, we aren't dying to ourselves and allowing our situations to bring that out of us. What happens all too often instead is we become more headstrong, wanting our way and feeling that it is our right. That's an intricate part of male-female dynamics, and when we live in a society that demands such, trust doesn't have room for entry anywhere in its ranks. Becoming a spouse – whether husband or wife to husband or wife – that allows his or her heart to trust therein, to trust beyond what they see and beyond any issues they may have – is one who has come to a place that God can truly work in an individual through their relationship.

Intimate relationships are about far more than procreation and legal sex. They are also about developing holiness, becoming something more than we are right now and learning how to properly interact with others through love. Oh yes, they are also about trust: trust in intimate places, trust in life, and proving that trust is something that changes the world, given we trust in right and trustworthy people.

- Day 53 -
Ready to be Blessed!

JABEZ CRIED TO THE GOD OF ISRAEL, SAYING, OH, THAT YOU WOULD BLESS ME
AND ENLARGE MY BORDER, AND THAT YOUR HAND MIGHT BE WITH ME, AND YOU WOULD KEEP
ME FROM EVIL SO IT MIGHT NOT HURT ME! AND GOD GRANTED HIS REQUEST.
(1 CHRONICLES 4:10)

READING: PSALM 103:1-13

ANY time I find a particularly stunning pair of shoes online, I am the first to ask for them as a blessing. I started this a few years ago when I noticed how interested people were in my shoes and in following them on social media. Keeping up with special footwear is a job in and of itself, and my budget often doesn't allow me to buy every pair of shoes I see or might like to see. I have also put myself on a limit, as buying so many shoes means you don't always have room to keep them somewhere. So, when I find a pair of shoes that meets the criteria and might work out well if someone gets the vibe, I post the shoes I find on Amazon on Facebook with a message: Someone please bless me! When I post, I do so fully well expecting to receive my shoe blessing. It might not come, but whether or not it does, I accept the result. I just do so expecting and trusting that blessing can come my way, and I put up the prayer that if this is a blessing for me, someone will respond.

Standing on blessing is something new to me as a person because blessings weren't something we thought to ask for, except in an abstract sense. When I was growing up, asking for a blessing meant going before a priest or other official minister of the church and receiving a prayer. That was the beginning and the end of it; nothing more, nothing else. The concept of being blessed by something material in nature was foreign and would probably equate to materialism in the mind's eye view. When I got older and was able to see that people were blessed by receiving things in the Bible, I changed my mind. I believe that, as with all things, there are middle points and balances we need to achieve to enjoy any blessing in our lives. It's wrong to think all blessings are material, but it's equally wrong to think blessings cannot touch our lives when they come through receipt of something this side of heaven. Sometimes the encouragement found in receiving a blessing transcends whatever need the material item might touch. It is possible to convey blessing through receipt of an object, just as it is possible to receive blessing without any object in sight.

Every one of us should be ready to be blessed. We should anticipate the blessing of God however He decides to send it to us. In our spiritual walk, we should attune ourselves to recognizing the things God does for us, every day and in every way, that touch our lives, our hearts, our minds, and bless us as individuals. In addition to being ready to be blessed, we should also be ready to be a blessing to someone else. Yes, receiving a blessing is great, but it's also important to be someone who echoes the love of God in their own lives and makes sure others are blessed, too. We aren't just blessed to receive; we are also blessed to pay it forward, as we like to say, and to give to someone else. We all know others have needs and need to feel that special touch of blessing. We can make it happen if we are only willing to let God work through us to that end.

Blessing isn't a one-time event; it is a circle, something that flows to us and then through us, completing the circle, finding its way all around, and then coming back to where it started. It's not an accident that God and eternity both are represented by a circle. In God, we find eternity, the blessing that never ends, and we become a part of that as we are willing to give and, yes, receive.

- Day 54 -
Adventures in Vacuuming

> OR WHAT KING, GOING OUT TO ENGAGE IN CONFLICT WITH ANOTHER KING, WILL NOT FIRST SIT DOWN AND CONSIDER *AND* TAKE COUNSEL WHETHER HE IS ABLE WITH TEN THOUSAND [MEN] TO MEET HIM WHO COMES AGAINST HIM WITH TWENTY THOUSAND? AND IF HE CANNOT [DO SO], WHEN THE OTHER KING IS STILL A GREAT WAY OFF, HE SENDS AN ENVOY AND ASKS THE TERMS OF PEACE.
> (LUKE 14:31-32)

READING: PROVERBS 29:22-27

I hate to clean the house. Cleaning is just not my thing. It feels like an exercise in futility, because that's exactly what it is. I can clean things up, only to find them dirty again in the not real distant future. That's aggravating to me. I acknowledge some cleaning is necessary, but I am not doing any more than I absolutely must. I'd rather do something, anything else. I used to feel guilty, because I knew so many people who seemed obsessively clean. They would spend hours keeping house every single day, and I just was so unwilling to do that. Now I realize being too clean is a compulsion in and of itself, and that makes me feel better as I sit amidst my overcrowded room that needs cleaning, but instead, I am writing devotions for this book.

There's one cleaning endeavor that has become an adventure in my house: vacuuming. The two reasons why vacuuming has become exciting: Fiona and Gideon.

I mentioned Fiona earlier in this book, well Gideon is my other dog. In every way possible, he is the opposite of Fiona. He is laid back and mostly quiet and is an extreme comfort to have around. Fiona is a little more difficult to handle. She talks back via barking and is always wanting to eat or chew on something, even now in her senior years. When it comes to vacuuming, however, they both get riled up in different ways. They can be sound asleep. They can be in another room. When that vacuum comes out, they are ready for action. Both dogs will bark at the vacuum, Fiona tries to attack the vacuum, Gideon runs and hides from the vacuum at a certain point in the process, and don't get me started on the wand or upholstery tools. Fiona feels such objects are a dire attack and she must, at any and all costs, get at them, even if they are in mid-air. The vacuum is the enemy, and both dogs have their own ways of handling it.

I have to admire Fiona's go get 'em attitude when it comes to the vacuum, even if it gets a bit annoying to handle after a few minutes. She is not afraid to confront what she perceives to be an enemy, but in the long run, it is just a perceived enemy. She's battling an object that has no interest in her, whatsoever. Her energy, her time, her thoughts are all channeled into an object that means her no harm and intends no battle. It's just there to clean no matter what she thinks of it. Even Gideon's retreat is admirable in the sense that he feels it's something he can't stand up to and has no desire to even try. He recognizes it's not a battle for him, but he still does not come to terms with what it's for or why we need it. He just keeps leaving it alone, to its own devices.

The lesson I've learned in this is quite simple: pick your battles. There are some battles we are so ready to go in and fight that aren't even real, and there are some battles we retreat from without considering the source in the first place. We should take the time to consider our course of action before impulsively going one way or another. It's easy to overreact and it's easy to retreat, but it's much harder to take the time to think about a battle plan prior to our work. Whether it's about housework, vacuuming, or something much deeper in our lives, our successes lie in our willingness to consider our actions, think about our plan, and stop barking long enough to hear God's direction about just what is needed, and when.

- Day 55 -
Kicking and Screaming

AND HAVE YOU [COMPLETELY] FORGOTTEN THE DIVINE WORD OF APPEAL
AND ENCOURAGEMENT IN WHICH YOU ARE REASONED WITH *AND* ADDRESSED AS SONS?
MY SON, DO NOT THINK LIGHTLY *OR* SCORN TO SUBMIT TO THE CORRECTION *AND* DISCIPLINE
OF THE LORD, NOR LOSE COURAGE *AND* GIVE UP *AND* FAINT WHEN YOU ARE REPROVED
OR CORRECTED BY HIM; FOR THE LORD CORRECTS *AND* DISCIPLINES EVERYONE WHOM
HE LOVES, AND HE PUNISHES, EVEN SCOURGES, EVERY SON WHOM HE ACCEPTS
AND WELCOMES TO HIS HEART *AND* CHERISHES. YOU MUST SUBMIT TO *AND* ENDURE
[CORRECTION] FOR DISCIPLINE; GOD IS DEALING WITH YOU AS WITH SONS. FOR WHAT SON
IS THERE WHOM HIS FATHER DOES NOT [THUS] TRAIN *AND* CORRECT *AND* DISCIPLINE?
NOW IF YOU ARE EXEMPT FROM CORRECTION *AND* LEFT WITHOUT DISCIPLINE IN WHICH
ALL [OF GOD'S CHILDREN] SHARE, THEN YOU ARE ILLEGITIMATE OFFSPRING
AND NOT TRUE SONS [AT ALL].
(HEBREWS 12:5-8)

READING: HEBREWS 12:10-25

My dog Gideon hates getting a bath. Such has been true since he was a puppy. When he was first brought home, he got a bath and fought in the tub the whole time. The older he's gotten the bigger he's gotten, and now he is a full-size, 80-pound Labrador Retriever who rejects a bath, every single time. No matter how hard we might try to get him in that bathtub, he wants no part of it. A usually complacent, easy-going animal becomes dead set on his way, even sticking his back legs out over the door posts, so no one can get him in that bathroom! Then while getting his bath, he pouts and is uncooperative until the entire ordeal is over.

Once I was asked, "Do you want to give Gideon a bath?" To which I replied, "I'd rather eat glass." That was no exaggeration, and my most definite sentiments on the whole matter. Gideon would go into the bath time experience kicking and screaming, and I, too, would go in kicking and screaming, just to avoid giving him a bath.

I realized the same about myself in a spiritual sense, not all that long ago. Recently, I walked away from something I'd been a part of since its inception, because I both covered the leader of the organization and the organization, as well. It hadn't been an experience that went ideally well…or ideally, at all. From day one, I set my sights to help make this thing work and do my best with it. Over time, one problem turned into another, which turned into another still, and the accountability that should have been present for such problems was just never there. I decided around August of last year that I was going to leave at the beginning of the year, and I was content with that decision. Yet, when the beginning of the year came, God wouldn't allow me to leave. Instead of being at peace with the decision to leave, God made me wait. He reminded me of my continued commitment to this work, and that I needed to see this through until the time was complete. He was also quick to assure me that when the time was complete, I would know.

I remained a part of the work kicking and screaming, the whole way. I was just like Gideon getting a bath: I wanted no part of it. Sometimes doing my duty or being on the job I was assigned to be a part of was agonizing. It wasn't what I wanted to do, or how I wanted to do it. I was ready to be done, but it didn't take too long before I realized staying, as I was, was required for a bigger purpose. I kicked and screamed my way through until the way was made – and was made easy – for my departure. Just as God promised, when the time came, I was uniquely aware it was time, and I needed to do what needed to be done in that moment to handle the situation and make my exit.

I am so grateful for the love of a God Who recognizes our difficulties and provides us His ample grace to get through our periods of "kicking and screaming." Just like Gideon reaches a point where he knows the bath is inevitable, so too do we realize our protests are going to be met with nothing but situations to obey God, no matter how much we might dislike having to hang on and do what we know He tells us to do. God knows what we don't, and our awareness of what we don't know needs to humble us to gain our composure, pull ourselves together, and silence our kicking and screaming until the opportunity arises to handle things as they need be, once and for all.

- Day 56 -
A Sabbath Rest for the Minister of God

AGAIN HE SETS A DEFINITE DAY, [A NEW] TODAY, [AND GIVES ANOTHER OPPORTUNITY OF SECURING THAT REST] SAYING THROUGH DAVID AFTER SO LONG A TIME IN THE WORDS ALREADY QUOTED, TODAY, IF YOU WOULD HEAR HIS VOICE *AND* WHEN YOU HEAR IT, DO NOT HARDEN YOUR HEARTS. [THIS MENTION OF A REST WAS NOT A REFERENCE TO THEIR ENTERING INTO CANAAN.] FOR IF JOSHUA HAD GIVEN THEM REST, HE [GOD] WOULD NOT SPEAK AFTERWARD ABOUT ANOTHER DAY. SO THEN, THERE IS STILL AWAITING A FULL *AND* COMPLETE SABBATH-REST RESERVED FOR THE [TRUE] PEOPLE OF GOD; FOR HE WHO HAS ONCE ENTERED [GOD'S] REST ALSO HAS CEASED FROM [THE WEARINESS AND PAIN] OF HUMAN LABORS, JUST AS GOD RESTED FROM THOSE LABORS PECULIARLY HIS OWN.
(HEBREWS 4:7-10)

READING: MATTHEW 11:27-30

LAST week, I found myself in quite a predicament: I got sick. It doesn't happen to me that often, but when it does, I tend to get so sick I am unable to do much. I typically land myself on the couch, coughing, snuffling, and exhausted until I can resume normal life. This isn't fun for me when it happens. I am a doer, and I like doing things to be productive and busy. I find my inspiration in doing, rather than laying around. As a result, I tend to exacerbate my early illness symptoms by working through them instead of resting. I would feel something coming on and cram as much into a day or two as possible, so I wouldn't miss out on anything. Then I'd lay around, sometimes sick as imaginable, for a week or two, because I was really sick by that point. It would be hard to restore health, and I'd cough for weeks after, because I had taxed my body to the point of total illness.

I decided to try something different this time, because I know I don't have the time, nor the desire, to spend several weeks sick. Instead of pushing myself, I started resting at the first hint I was not feeling well. I took some time and rested, taking what the Bible speaks of as a "Sabbath rest." I set aside so many days and relaxed my body, resting and hand sewing to take some time to avoid further infection, and it worked. In resting and taking the time to rest, my body healed itself much faster, and I did not become nearly as sick as I ordinarily would have become.

Rest is not always what I might like to do, but that does not make it any less necessary. Being a Christian means adopting the lifestyle of a mover and a shaker. We should never be people who like to let grass grow under our feet, nor should we be willing to take a back seat while others do things we can do. Rest, however, is something necessary in the life of each and every believer. It is so important of a principle it is found from Genesis to Revelation, first as the Sabbath day in the Old Testament, and now as the Sabbath rest promised to the people of God in the New Testament. This doesn't mean we are required to observe Saturday as the Sabbath day, but that we are to be people who follow the leading of the Spirit to find our rest in Christ, our purpose in Him and our cycles of rest and labor in His leading.

The principle of "Sabbath rest" is a Biblical pointing to the time after Jesus returns and the world shall dwell in perfect harmony, as we worship God and cease eternal labors in the presence of our God and Savior. It's a concept that, if we are honest with ourselves, is probably hard to imagine. We are so used to our work cycles and our labors, the concept of "Sabbath rest" might sound like an endless parade or vacation. This is not what it is at all, however. Being sick proved to me that rest in God is different from the time we take to amuse and entertain ourselves. Rest is about rest, not entertainment. It is learning to move slower, observe our own cycles and habits, and come to a point where the focus of God is more valuable to us than our own vain attempts to try and bring about change and enjoyment to pass ourselves. In

Sabbath rest, we find a new place of worship as we connect ourselves to the One Who created us and see ourselves as a part of Him rather than trying to fit Him in as a part of our pre-existing schedules that move along at their own hurrying pace. When we slow down, we see God first, rather than last or secondary.

- Day 57 -
Happiness is...

HAPPY ARE YOUR WIVES *AND* MEN, AND HAPPY ARE THESE YOUR SERVANTS WHO STAND
CONTINUALLY BEFORE YOU AND HEAR YOUR WISDOM!
(2 CHRONICLES 9:7)

READING: PSALM 1:1-6

WHEN Macy's "Celebrate" commercial launched, the song made me want to get up and dance, church style. When I looked up the lyrics, I noted they all center around the line: "You'll never feel happy/Oh no you won't/Until you try." They took me back to a project I did in third grade where we read the book, *Happiness Is...* and then had to make our own books that told what happiness was to us. It was a great project, because it showed us happiness in a way we could understand as kids. We were easily able to correlate happiness with things we did or received, and in a strange way, it taught us that happiness is something that's just...not...permanent.

I started thinking about this project in correlation with the commercial and it crossed my mind: when in our lives did we start thinking happiness was something we should just have, permanently? At some point between that third grade project and our current age, we got a very different message about happiness. We started thinking happiness is something we should have all the time. Happiness has become about lifestyle entitlement rather than our choices, and we are quick and fast to protest whenever we feel we aren't happy. We expect being unhappy to rate a response and things line up quickly, and when it doesn't happen, we grow more unhappy.

There's some truth to what they sing about in the Macy's commercial: we won't feel happy until we try. To try, we must understand how happiness works and what brings happiness into our lives. Foundationally, the Bible never promises us that we will be happy constantly. In fact, the Bible proves happiness to be a cause-and-effect thing: something happens, we are happy about it as a result, and our state of happiness is directly tied to whatever made us happy. This also means happiness is fleeting. It comes and goes with the circumstances that cause us to feel that way.

If we are looking for life to make us happy all the time, we are going to be unhappy. We're missing the point if we think happiness is the goal of our lives. The mere fact that it comes and goes with situations should prove to us it's not something we should pursue, day in and day out, as our life pursuit. Instead of focusing so much on happiness, the Bible encourages us to pursue the fullness of joy. Joy and happiness are quite different; while happiness is circumstantial, joy is based on a confident assurance of purpose and peace, one that reminds us of greater things to achieve than personal satisfaction. The funny thing about joy is while it's not all about us, it is something that does lead us to a place where we find the satisfaction we seek in our lives. If we aren't chasing something that's all about us (happiness), we can finally relax and take our rightful place in life.

We will never grow as people if we don't step up and accept a few things about happiness. Happiness isn't permanent, but we will never find any form of it if we don't try. We will also never be happy if it's all we think we need in this life. We will find a better state of happiness, however, if we are willing to find joy and bring some stability into our circumstances and inner dialogue. The promise of future joy, of hope, and yes, even of happiness, can't rest and reside on the foundations of happiness itself. If we stop seeking to be happy, we will find different things that bring us true and lasting joy, and we will find that key...if we only give God's spiritual principles a try.

- DAY 58 -
Love and Eternity

AND SO FAITH, HOPE, LOVE ABIDE [FAITH—CONVICTION AND BELIEF RESPECTING MAN'S RELATION TO GOD AND DIVINE THINGS; HOPE—JOYFUL AND CONFIDENT EXPECTATION OF ETERNAL SALVATION; LOVE—TRUE AFFECTION FOR GOD AND MAN, GROWING OUT OF GOD'S LOVE FOR AND IN US], THESE THREE; BUT THE GREATEST OF THESE IS LOVE. EAGERLY PURSUE *AND* SEEK TO ACQUIRE [THIS] LOVE [MAKE IT YOUR AIM, YOUR GREAT QUEST]...
(1 CORINTHIANS 13:13-14:1)

READING: LUKE 6:27-36

WHEN I first got the vision for what is now Sanctuary International Fellowship Tabernacle – SIFT, its basic premise was the work of love and loving other people without politics or church polarities interfering in that process. It sounded like an easy concept, but through this work, I discovered just how controversial love remains. It is still the single most threatening force out there, because love itself is eternal. It brings us back home to our own mortality in this life; the finiteness of our own existence without God; and it reminds us that when all is said and done, all the things we have worked the hardest for won't be around that long after each of us dies.

There is only one thing now that we have the capacity to do into the next life, and that is love. Whether it's life after death in heaven or the return of Christ, we will love God, love one another, love our surroundings, and come to a fullness of the understanding in loving ourselves. There will be no shortage of this eternal promise, that is for sure! Where it seems like we lack love in this life and do not rightly understand which way to turn to find it in a deeper way, what we will find in the world to come will more than compensate for whatever is missing now.

The major difference between then and now will be our realization of love as the true extension of God it should be. There will be no question as to the way that love transforms and influences our lives. Where we now see division, it will be no longer. The reflection of us in God's image and the Spirit of God permeating and transforming us in the blink of an eye will make us realize, for real and in a tangible way, that love is just as real and incredible as we've always spoken about it.

Here, now, we often restrict love to a nice musing for marriage or intimate relationships. Seldom do we, even in church, work to apply love in a general sense beyond this one setting. We're still hung up and stuck on love as a principle of romance and excitement that then leads to children; we have not delved out yet into the realm of loving those closest and most immediate to us. In other words, we haven't stopped learning about loving those who are not an extension of ourselves. When the Scriptures teach us about loving our neighbors, regardless of who they are or what they are, it is challenging us to go beyond that which is temporal, or fleshly, and dive into a picture of eternity. It's easy to love those who are a part of us, or we of them; it is much harder, however, to love those who are very different. This is why love is eternal; it loves beyond the comfortable, easy borders and touches something different in each of us, that taps into the love God has for all of us.

Whenever we make that point to love others, especially those who are not of us, we are showing a picture of eternity, right now. It reveals the heart of God, one that cares for our every need and shows us that glimmer of hope of things to one day improve and be better. Still, we don't have to wait for the great beyond for things to be better. Love is the force behind any positive and enriching relationship, because it has the power to change even the hardest, empty heart. We might not understand it and we certainly don't always walk in it in the way we should, but love is God's most perfect gift to us. How do I know this? It has changed each and every one of us...or it should, if we allow it to flow into our lives.

- DAY 59 -
Community

AND LET US CONSIDER *AND* GIVE ATTENTIVE, CONTINUOUS CARE TO WATCHING OVER ONE ANOTHER, STUDYING HOW WE MAY STIR UP (STIMULATE AND INCITE) TO LOVE *AND* HELPFUL DEEDS *AND* NOBLE ACTIVITIES, NOT FORSAKING *OR* NEGLECTING TO ASSEMBLE TOGETHER [AS BELIEVERS], AS IS THE HABIT OF SOME PEOPLE, BUT ADMONISHING (WARNING, URGING, AND ENCOURAGING) ONE ANOTHER, AND ALL THE MORE FAITHFULLY AS YOU SEE THE DAY APPROACHING.
(HEBREWS 10:24-25)

READING: ACTS 4:32-37

UNITY has come up in this book a few times because it's been a running theme throughout my current season. When I first started in ministry, I branded as a "unity ministry." One of my core themes was unity within the church and, in a larger sense, sometimes unity in a worldly sense. Over the years, I came to see how unreasonable a goal it was in a worldly sense, because I came to a better spiritual understanding about who and what we should unite to – and who we should avoid in unity, as well. Even though I abandoned it as a precept for many years, I have come to see why unity is so important, especially in the life of the church. Where there is no unity there is no force for work, and one of the reasons we are lacking so much in church today is because we have no concept of community or working in a community setting.

Ask ten different people what community is and you will get ten different answers. One may say that a community is a group working toward a goal. Another may say that community is a formalized group of people, like a local church or neighborhood watch. Yet another may say that a community is an informal group of people with similar interests. Is this all community really is? Is it just the way we organize ourselves for reaching goals? Is it nothing more than formalized institutions? I say no, community is more than this. To discover such, all we need to do is look at the first-century church, especially as it was forming.

The community of believers who first followed Jesus were quite a group, especially from the outside looking in. At first glance, they looked very mismatched. They came from all different walks of life and had different occupations and personalities. Look at the first twelve apostles: Simon-Peter, Andrew, James the Greater, and John were fishermen; Matthew was a tax-collector; Simon was a Jewish Zealot; Philip and Bartholomew had unknown positions; Thomas was a doubter; and Judas, the one who was most stellar with money, was both a treasurer and a traitor. Could Jesus have picked a more different group of men? Yet despite their differences, they were a community that helped to form an even larger one: the early church, the first Christians. To move down to where we are today might seem like a slow process, but the entirety of church history begins and moves forward today with community.

Did the community Jesus started have a goal? Yes, the Kingdom of God. Was the community formalized? Yes and no. They weren't "formal" like we identify such today, but they had a set purpose and identity that they discovered more and more over time. Were they informal? Yes, as they were nothing more than a bunch of people who loved God and wanted to discover more about serving and loving Him.

I think the common link we often miss in our definition of community is found in God. With God, all things are possible, and this includes our attempts at working together and co-unifying for His purposes. It takes a community of believers to bring the Good News to the whole world, and we cannot have the Kingdom without the community. The one thing that united the first believers wasn't their brilliant thoughts or ideas of formalization, and it certainly wasn't their charismatic personalities. It was God, their love of God, and their focus that He was the only answer to transform anything and everything that will receive His touch.

- Day 60 -
Be on Your Guard Against Men

BEHOLD, I SEND YOU FORTH AS SHEEP IN THE MIDST OF WOLVES: BE YE THEREFORE WISE AS SERPENTS, AND HARMLESS AS DOVES. BUT BEWARE OF MEN: FOR THEY WILL DELIVER YOU UP TO THE COUNCILS, AND THEY WILL SCOURGE YOU IN THEIR SYNAGOGUES; AND YE SHALL BE BROUGHT BEFORE GOVERNORS AND KINGS FOR MY SAKE, FOR A TESTIMONY AGAINST THEM AND THE GENTILES. BUT WHEN THEY DELIVER YOU UP, TAKE NO THOUGHT HOW OR WHAT YE SHALL SPEAK: FOR IT SHALL BE GIVEN YOU IN THAT SAME HOUR WHAT YE SHALL SPEAK. FOR IT IS NOT YE THAT SPEAK, BUT THE SPIRIT OF YOUR FATHER WHICH SPEAKETH IN YOU.
(MATTHEW 10:16-20, KJV)

READING: MICAH 7:5-9

A popular church trend for the past few years is the emphasis on relationships over principle. What this means is we encourage people to remain connected to individuals for the sake of connection, rather than examining who is right for us and whether we should attach ourselves to certain people in the first place. We claim this is done in the name of unity or in understanding unity, but the reality behind this avoids true unity because it's done under the guise of human vanity and concepts. We don't teach people to exercise good judgment or any variety of spiritual gifts we may cheerlead because doing so will mean many will walk away from things that those who influence us want us to remain connected. Such isn't Biblical, regardless, and one of the most powerful ways it proves unbiblical is found when Jesus Himself tells us to "be on your guard against men."

Hmmm. Let's think about this one. I'll set the stage Sophia (from *The Golden Girls*) style: Picture it. Galilee. Around 31 AD. Twelve men and women of varying ages, backgrounds, educations and positions gather around their teacher, Jesus Christ. He tells them to go out, two by two, with a list of specified commands: Heal the sick. Raise the dead. Cast out demons. Heal those with leprosy. Freely you have received, freely give. Don't take extra money or extra supplies. Remain where you stay, giving your greeting where you go. If those who are there reject you, leave that place and shake the dust off your feet. In describing the works they will do and the way they should do them, Jesus awakens within the possibility of reality: imprisonment. Death. Rejection. Disaster. The way He summed it up is found in one singular sentence: Be on your guard against men.

What does a statement like this mean to you? Some mothers tell their daughters things like this all the time: "Be on your guard. Don't let him touch you!" "Don't let him near you!" "Don't go with him in his car!" I don't think generations of mothering advice to their daughters is what Jesus meant, though. We never tell ourselves to be on guard against men, probably because we equate guardedness with a whole conglomerate of different things: mistrust, anger, hate, and evil, to say a few. Jesus never accused anyone we should beware of any of these things, did He? Jesus did not say be on your guard against a specific type of person. He never labeled those we are to beware as evil men, or difficult men, or hateful men, or angry men, but all men, and by extension, all people. We must know who to trust and who not to trust, and this is not always easily identifiable by the disguise they wrap themselves in. In His one sentence, Jesus tells us to beware anyone; to guard our hearts and spiritual lives with caution, and be careful who we trust, regardless of who they appear to be.

Jesus' words to us don't mean we should never trust or open up to anyone. We must develop conviction through discernment and find the necessary balance on this issue as much as any others we develop within ourselves. Conviction is being assured of the need to be guarded and following those spiritual instincts placed within us by God. It's a sign we trust in Him, because without conviction we either trust everybody or nobody. These six words given by Jesus were probably among the strongest admonition to caution and wisdom we can apply today, living in faith and trust of God first, and remaining cautious as to who influences and guides us today.

- Day 61 -
Hearing God's Voice

CALL TO ME AND I WILL ANSWER YOU AND SHOW YOU GREAT AND MIGHTY THINGS,
FENCED IN *AND* HIDDEN, WHICH YOU DO NOT KNOW (DO NOT DISTINGUISH AND RECOGNIZE,
HAVE KNOWLEDGE OF AND UNDERSTAND).
(JEREMIAH 33:3)

READING: 1 JOHN 1:1-7

As I write this, I have been in ministry for almost 20 years and a practicing, Spirit-filled Christian for 18 of those years. It might sound odd to have ministry experience prior, but remember, I have been in church a good part of my life. I knew I wanted to be in ministry even before I was born again. Over the years, I have always known and heard God's inward witness and His voice speaking to me. As I have grown in Him, however, the way I hear from God has radically changed. At first, I wasn't sure what I was experiencing. In the beginning, I thought God sounded a lot like me and what I had to say. Some of the leadings I experienced early on in hindsight sounded a lot more like me and what I wanted to do than God's principles at work in my life. Over time, I gained the insight and discernment to hear God speak to me and to lead me into the paths He desired me to take. Obeying was another story, but learning to recognize God's voice has always been an important part of my own personal journey.

As I have gone through this season, hearing God's voice has changed in a certain sense for me. It's not that it's different or I didn't hear from Him in the past; it's that the leading has a different sense of feel to it. It's a different sort of prompting and leading, and it has a much deeper rooting than in years past. It makes me realize that many who speak of hearing from God are doing what I did in my early years: they might have heard some from God, but they heard it through themselves. When we pass ourselves off as the voice of God, we never learn to hear from Him properly. It misleads other people as to the realness of His voice in our world, right now.

God's living, active voice is heard today, just as much as it was in days gone by. The principle of hearing from God is just as real as it was in Biblical times. God has things to say to us about where we are now and what we experience right now, and He wants you to listen. It's that simple, just like talking to anyone else and having a real and meaningful conversation with a trusted friend. This is the listening side of something we call "prayer," something often missing and lacking from our spiritual experiences. It is, nonetheless, of vital importance as we grow in Christ.

To hear from God, we must stop talking so much. Just like we talk in any situation, it is our heart's contentment to control and dominate conversations. We talk about prayer in a deep sense or as if it's some sort of formal recital before God, but every time we get on this intense soap box, we are ignoring the listening aspect of prayer and spiritual communication. Without listening, prayer is only half a communication and becomes too much about us and the things we are focused on rather than becoming God-centered and using prayer as a means to do that.

Are we searching for God, or are we searching for ourselves? Are we looking to hear from God and let Him transform us, or are we hoping we can pass off a version of ourselves as being divine and spiritually sound? We must seek God because we love Him, not because we want Him to become a big, validating version of us. We must long to listen to His voice, speaking to us, and the words that bring us life and health. He will help us on our journey and reveal marvelous things, if we are only ready and waiting to receive His wisdom within ourselves. When we seek God, we will find Him. His voice will lead our way, and He will reveal Himself to us.

- DAY 62 -
Standing Through the Things That Have no Answer

BEAR (ENDURE, CARRY) ONE ANOTHER'S BURDENS *AND* TROUBLESOME MORAL FAULTS,
AND IN THIS WAY FULFILL *AND* OBSERVE PERFECTLY THE LAW OF CHRIST (THE MESSIAH)
AND COMPLETE WHAT IS LACKING [IN YOUR OBEDIENCE TO IT]. FOR IF ANY PERSON THINKS
HIMSELF TO BE SOMEBODY [TOO IMPORTANT TO CONDESCEND TO SHOULDER ANOTHER'S
LOAD] WHEN HE IS NOBODY [OF SUPERIORITY EXCEPT IN HIS OWN ESTIMATION],
HE DECEIVES *AND* DELUDES *AND* CHEATS HIMSELF.
(GALATIANS 6:2-3)

READING: ROMANS 12:10-18

THE season one, episode eight airing of the show *Star* was titled "Mama's Boy." In the episode is a dramatic depiction of a control-based attempt at "deliverance" of Cotton, the transgender daughter (born Arnold) of Carlotta. The show depicts Carlotta as a strong, church-going Christian hairdresser whose faith guides her through much of her life. The story of her faith is complicated, however, because it shows her own temptations, particularly in her attraction to her pastor, with whom she is intimately involved. Carlotta and Cotton do not see eye-to-eye because of Cotton's gender identity and the complicated and complex loss it caused Carlotta, as she feels she lost her son. More than just a personal loss, Carlotta doesn't understand Cotton's difficulties and journeys as a transgender individual and strongly disagrees with Cotton's life as a prostitute and escort. Their relationship issues intensify when Carlotta calls upon her pastor to try and help her and Cotton with their problems, only for him to turn the entire thing into a cruel and controlling casting out session, accusing Cotton of having a demon. The whole ordeal ends with Cotton contemplating suicide and Carlotta throwing the pastor out of the house. Cotton believed her mother had set her up, while the show indicates she didn't anticipate the mess going as far and into as invasive territory as the pastor chose to go.

As I watched the episode with my mother, her clear and unequivocal response was: "That was wrong. What that man did was wrong." She also identified that this is one of those very difficult issues for people that doesn't seem to have a good answer. Those who experience it struggle to find themselves and their voice, to make their physical bodies align with what they recognize within themselves, and those who are around them often struggle to understand something that doesn't seem to have an easy answer. The pastor represented the view the church (and many even outside of the church) desire to take on topics like this: they want the easy way out. They want to scream and shout at people, call people names, demean what people do and what they go through, they take no consideration for people's feelings, and many hope – and believe – the issues will be easily solved with such an approach.

What I got out of watching that episode of *Star* aligned with my mom's thoughts, but in a different way. It's often assumed that in ministry, we are here as a divine "answer council." People come to us thinking we have all the answers to life, and we can explain anything and everything because we are leaders of faith. It's believed we can make anything change or go away with simplistic methods and that everything can be clearer and easy if we do it hard enough or long enough. This is a misnomer, however. It's not as simple to say we can just make the hard questions or situations go away, because the truth is we don't have answers for all of them. There are many things we don't understand or know, and will never know, because they aren't things that are answerable. Some things just are. Some things have no explanation. They just are, due to no fault of anyone involved or of any doing on anyone's part. If we call ourselves people of faith, it is our position to stand with people through the hard things, through the things that have no explanation, to offer support and strength as they come to terms with reality, and divine hope, rather than promoting what might seem most easy.

- DAY 63 -
Don't Let Me Get Me

> FOR I DO NOT UNDERSTAND MY OWN ACTIONS [I AM BAFFLED, BEWILDERED]. I DO NOT PRACTICE *OR* ACCOMPLISH WHAT I WISH, BUT I DO THE VERY THING THAT I LOATHE [WHICH MY MORAL INSTINCT CONDEMNS]. NOW IF I DO [HABITUALLY] WHAT IS CONTRARY TO MY DESIRE, [THAT MEANS THAT] I ACKNOWLEDGE *AND* AGREE THAT THE LAW IS GOOD (MORALLY EXCELLENT) *AND* THAT I TAKE SIDES WITH IT. HOWEVER, IT IS NO LONGER I WHO DO THE DEED, BUT THE SIN [PRINCIPLE] WHICH IS AT HOME IN ME *AND* HAS POSSESSION OF ME. FOR I KNOW THAT NOTHING GOOD DWELLS WITHIN ME, THAT IS, IN MY FLESH. I CAN WILL WHAT IS RIGHT, BUT I CANNOT PERFORM IT. [I HAVE THE INTENTION AND URGE TO DO WHAT IS RIGHT, BUT NO POWER TO CARRY IT OUT.] FOR I FAIL TO PRACTICE THE GOOD DEEDS I DESIRE TO DO, BUT THE EVIL DEEDS THAT I DO NOT DESIRE TO DO ARE WHAT I AM [EVER] DOING.
> (ROMANS 7:15-19)

READING: GALATIANS 5:16-21

ONCE awhile back I was teaching a Bible Study at Sanctuary International Fellowship Tabernacle – SIFT and the topic of enemies came up. We wound up discussing the question of enemies: what is an enemy and what makes someone an enemy? One woman posed the very poignant question, "Do any of us really have enemies?" I later taught during our Sunday service about Satan, who manipulates people and situations to get us into a frenzy and upset so we won't follow God as we should. He is our true enemy, but we often find others to do his bidding in this world, thus becoming our enemies, as well.

We could have easily spent an entire Bible study series exploring different types of enemies as existed in the Bible. If that was our desired focus, there probably wouldn't have been room for much else, because it would have sent us on a path of life examination to the point where we were uncomfortable with anyone else we might have known. I cut the teaching off because such thoughts often lead from one thing to another and can lead us away from what we should be looking at. There was one enemy we didn't talk about, and that enemy was us, ourselves.

Social media has fed our desire to indulge in the idea that we are sufficient as we are and those who dislike us have no reason to do so. We are quick to look around and see so many things around us that upset us, bother us, and come against us. Meme after meme focuses on those who seem to be against whatever they don't like about us. It's easy to focus on those people and those issues as our ultimate obstacles. We love to talk about getting around our haters and enemies, as if eliminating them from our lives will really accomplish something.

Sure, it might do something for a little while. The stress of having someone oppose us may alleviate initially, but what happens when we reach the point where our realities stare us in the face? Where do we look in the mirror and the fact that we are standing right where we were a year ago, and two years ago, and five years ago, and maybe ten or more years ago, with no change, hit us in the face? At that moment, it's not our haters, nor our outside enemies we must examine. It is us, the very essence of who we are, and how we are literally standing in our own way as God tries to work within us, but we fight it at every turn.

Yes, Satan is our enemy. Yes, Satan works through others who become enemies. Yes, we must fight against the opposition that others bring into our lives and the difficulties that come along with it. We can spend our entire lives thinking everyone else is our problem and fighting with others to try and get where we want to get. We will never accomplish anything, except to make many enemies and isolate ourselves. When we are real with ourselves and admit the greatest enemy we will ever fight as we go along in this walk is ourselves, we will accomplish a huge victory. We must fight our desires and temptations that threaten our futures and the sins that keep us away from God. Forever we will fight against our own will, our own stubbornness that insists on going our own way, and the many ways that we miss God within ourselves. We can't let ourselves get ourselves because we are too busy looking at everyone else around us. Let go of the wrongs and focus on where God needs you to be.

- Day 64 -
Breaking the Habit

EVERYTHING IS PERMISSIBLE (ALLOWABLE AND LAWFUL) FOR ME; BUT NOT ALL THINGS
ARE HELPFUL (GOOD FOR ME TO DO, EXPEDIENT AND PROFITABLE WHEN CONSIDERED
WITH OTHER THINGS). EVERYTHING IS LAWFUL FOR ME, BUT I WILL NOT BECOME THE SLAVE
OF ANYTHING *OR* BE BROUGHT UNDER ITS POWER.
(1 CORINTHIANS 6:12)

READING: 2 TIMOTHY 1:6-10

ON the first season finale of the show *This Is Us*, a flashback featuring Jack and Rebecca reveals an intense fight the two had before separating. Their three kids were teenagers by this point in time. They had been having different marital issues for some time before they had this intense fight. During the argument, Jack attempts to tell Rebecca how much he loves her when she asks the question, "What is it that you love about me?" He couldn't answer the question off the cuff. She pointed out that he told her he loves her out of habit, rather than out of a real genuine feel and love for her as a person. This comment made me think about all the things we do or say out of nothing more than habit, and how bad it can be to do that.

About three weeks ago, I had a very bad day. I was very upset with the state of ministry as it is and some of the situations I am in because of the sacrifices I have had to make to pursue ministry without the needed commitment from those who claim to be a part of this ministry. When someone asked me how my day was, I didn't respond with an enthusiastic church cheer. I broke the habit, the temptation to act like everything is perfect because I am in ministry, and I told the truth that I wasn't having a good day, and why. The person responded to me by saying, "God is in control."

I hit the roof because that was a completely insensitive answer. He gave no comfort or words of assurance and did nothing to say, "I'm sorry you are having a bad day." When I didn't respond with typical church-like responses, this man was confused. He couldn't figure out why I did not readily receive what he said, and went as far as to call it insincere and say he didn't care. He felt that because he responded as people always do, it should have been enough...even though it wasn't.

He was responding not out of genuine concern or care, but out of habit. That was what I felt from him, and that was how it sounded. It was just a string of things to say to make one sound churchy rather than sincere, and it was a way to placate other people into feeling like they were being heard when they were not. When confronted with someone who saw through that and called out the habit, he didn't know, nor understand how to break it.

Habits are things we do repeatedly, over and over again, without thinking about them. If we are honest with ourselves, we do many, many things out of habit in the Name of God that have become a comfortable part of our tradition and our concepts of how we should interact with others. In church, we say things like "Praise the Lord!" and "I'm blessed and highly favored!" for no other reason than we have been taught they are what we think we are supposed to say. If someone responds with anything else, no matter what their circumstances are, we automatically assume they don't have as much faith as we do. We're quick to judge, slow to listen, and almost nonexistent to care about the issues others may have.

Love should never be associated with habit, whether it is in the sense of marriage, as Jack and Rebecca showed us on television, or in our interactions with other individuals. If we are to impact others, we need to convey genuine care rather than automatically responding to others from our vast bank of cliché programming.

- DAY 65 -
It Rains on the Just and Unjust Alike

TO SHOW THAT YOU ARE THE CHILDREN OF YOUR FATHER WHO IS IN HEAVEN;
FOR HE MAKES HIS SUN RISE ON THE WICKED AND ON THE GOOD, AND MAKES THE RAIN FALL
UPON THE UPRIGHT AND THE WRONGDOERS [ALIKE].
(MATTHEW 5:45)

READING: MATTHEW 7:1-6

THROUGHOUT my former season, I saw people come and go, as well as seeing things quickly turn and change for people. It was a period of great tumult, not just for me, but for others around me, too. Some people came to a point of great breakthroughs, while others experienced great trials. I think it's safe to say that even though I saw this season as my own, it ran concurrently with the seasons others encountered through that time. None of us were the same when our seasons changed and turned, because none of us are who we used to be back then. Good things happened, and bad things happened.

Personally, I had a mixed season. It wasn't all bad. I made some great strides and had some awesome victories, but it wasn't all fun and games. I had my losses and my heartache, and they came more frequently than that which felt good or rated a positive experience. And yes, I was one to look over the victories of others at times and wonder why something good was happening to some people. I decided they weren't good people and, therefore, nothing good should happen to them.

Can anyone say...judgment? This is exactly what it is when we make this sort of a statement or harbor these thoughts. It's more than jealousy or envy; it's a real question that we ask when we can't make sense of the bad they've done and the results they got, mixed with the good we've done and the bad results we have. When we decide someone else shouldn't have something because of who we feel they are, it is a judgment on our part. We make the judgment to make sure our world makes sense, that our paradigm is in place, and we sit there...angry...because someone got something and we don't think they should have it. Maybe it's more accurate to say we think we should have it, or have it differently, than we do, and we are upset over that, so we judge what others have. That's never a wise move, but it's real and honest to admit it is something that's a part of the human condition as we attempt to figure out this thing called life.

It's tempting to look out over the landscape of our lives and wonder why good things happen to bad people. In our realm of immature faith, we assume only good things should happen to those who make the effort to be good. Bad things should happen to those who are bad; not those who are good. When bad things happen to good people and good things happen to bad people, we get confused. We don't know what to make of it. It threatens our entire equilibrium of sense and reason. It assaults what we think we know about ourselves and others, and the call to be good or bad.

One of the major problems with this logic is that God never promised salvation was to make good people better or fix bad people. It exists to connect us to God. When the Bible tells us it rains on the just and unjust alike, that means everything we know and think about good things as a reward and bad things as a punishment must be discarded, as hard as that is for us to fathom. Good things happen and bad things happen, and God is in them all, speaking to the good and bad alike, and reaching out in the hopes that He will reach every one of us for His glory. In life, we will experience the good and the bad, as the host of experiences transforms us to see the hand of God and recognize His presence in every situation, whether we like it, or not.

- DAY 66 -
What's Really Important

FOR WHERE YOUR TREASURE IS, THERE WILL YOUR HEART BE ALSO.
(LUKE 12:34)

READING: MATTHEW 6:31-34

LAST year, I was approached by an individual in Pakistan who wanted me to start a branch of Sanctuary International Fellowship Tabernacle – SIFT in Lahore. This was a huge undertaking for me, but I was willing to do it, because they indicated they were willing to assume the costs. A scan through Facebook photos indicated there was money to keep up with high fashion trends, expensive hair products, and personal property, so that told me the money was there for the project. When push came to shove, the project didn't come to fruition, under the guise of no money. When I pointed out there was money for other things, the individual got angry with me.

There's a chant I hear all the time: "I can't afford it!" It doesn't matter what it is. It can be education, a book, a conference, buying an item, services, or something else of that nature – they can't afford it. They might want it for free, but they make it really clear they just don't have it in their budget to cover it. There's often a long, sorted explanation with the statement, something to the extent of why their finances are overextended and why it's just not an option for them right now. If you give them the option to do it later, most don't ever get back with you to take it. Something else comes up and something else comes along, and whatever it was that they wanted seems about as relevant as it did when it first came up. Time and time again, things pass, things move along, and whatever they claim to want just never seems to catch up.

Whenever we read Bible passages about money, we tend to trip spiritually. The passages don't seem to go along with Jesus, Who appears to have done many miracles and healings without cost, and Who appears to have taught for free wherever He went. We get uncomfortable when words about money and the realities therein came from the mouth of this same individual. Surely that's a confusion or a mistake, right? Wrong! Jesus might not have charged a formalized fee, but He did have a treasurer, who handled the donations and offerings for the work. People who received from His ministry were expected to give, because they were prompted and moved to do so by God. Those who received them were expected to do the right thing, because they received the right thing. It moved in a circle, one that echoes the movements of eternity, and things found their way back that the Word would not return void. Jesus' purpose in teaching us about money was to drive home the reality that how we spend our money relates to our character. It wouldn't work for Him to teach about character and spiritual relationship without dealing with our spending habits, because what we are willing to spend our money on – and not spend our money on – says a lot about us as people.

When the Bible teaches us that wherever our treasure is, there our heart is, too, it wasn't telling us everything in our lives relates to money or should relate to money. Jesus was telling us if you want to know what is most important in someone's life, follow their money. It's not that we can't afford things; it is that those are not the things we make as our first priority. We can say with our mouths that God comes first, and we are all about the Kingdom, but what makes that statement true or untrue is how much we give toward advancing God's work. If you don't want to do something, be upfront about that – but stop saying you can't afford it. If you can afford everything else, the issue isn't your finances, it's your heart.

- Day 67 -
Whatever...

THEN THE LORD ANSWERED JOB OUT OF THE WHIRLWIND AND SAID, WHO IS THIS THAT
DARKENS COUNSEL BY WORDS WITHOUT KNOWLEDGE? GIRD UP NOW YOUR LOINS
LIKE A MAN, AND I WILL DEMAND OF YOU, AND YOU DECLARE TO ME.
(JOB 38:1-3)

READING: LUKE 17:11-19

ONE of the most common aspects of Christian interaction on social media is the prayer request. If people know you are a minister, odds are good they will hit you up via inbox for prayer. Nobody ever follows up when a request is answered or if they want to discuss it further. The only time you hear from them is when they are looking for something and they expect you to drop everything and pray for them.

I've never been a person who believes in the need to pray specific prayers for everyone who comes and asks for them. I think there is more than one way to covet someone's time or attention and asking for prayer without ever giving anything back or offering anything in return is a sign of the greed we have in church today. The consideration that maybe you need something, or you simply do not have time to pay attention to their needs is just not there. It doesn't help that many of these issues are repeat issues and some use them to get attention from others under the guise of prayer. I believe we should pray for others; I believe we should care enough to pray for others; but getting to the nitty gritty specifications of everyone's prayer interests, requests, and the details of the results they want from your prayers isn't something we are called to do for every single person who contacts us with a prayer request.

When I get requests like this, especially from people I don't know very well, their prayers go into a general prayer discussion I have with God. I'll be talking to Him and say, "OK God, whatever…" and in that statement, God knows what I am talking about. "Whatever…" is my general cue for each and every prayer request that I do not have time, nor sometimes the interest, nor the memory, to mention specifically. By telling God "Whatever," I am releasing those needs into His hands, the ones He knows those people need (and sometimes my own), and the spiritual insights and needs we all need to receive.

The older I get, the fuller my time is, the less time I have to listen to every set of need and nonsense that cross my path, the more I realize some things just don't rate a response; they rate a "whatever…" For many years of my life, I took on every cause and issue that came across my desk…or my life…or my feed. I was quick to empathize and a little too eager to give people the benefit of the doubt. Nowadays, I wonder how many other people have heard this story, or this request, or this situation, and the issue still hasn't been resolved, because the person who is being prayed for isn't changing. Yes, we all need others to pray for us, but that should be something mutual. It shouldn't be that we are always praying for people who never seem to get better or lift themselves out of the situations they find themselves in.

None of us can expect others to care about our situations as much as we do. When we make that kind of demand, we rate a "whatever…" because we must step up to the plate and take ourselves to the throne to get the insight and answers we need. We need to care enough to pray our way through, ask trusted people to pray for us and with us when it is truly necessary, and gather up ourselves as spiritually growing individuals to become more than just a name and a face in the crowd. God can do amazing things within us, but we must be willing to do the work. Prayer doesn't change God; it changes you and me, as we are willing to yield to His hand.

- Day 68 -
You Lie Like a Rug on the Floor

WE HAVE RENOUNCED DISGRACEFUL WAYS (SECRET THOUGHTS, FEELINGS, DESIRES AND UNDERHANDEDNESS, THE METHODS AND ARTS THAT MEN HIDE THROUGH SHAME); WE REFUSE TO DEAL CRAFTILY (TO PRACTICE TRICKERY AND CUNNING) OR TO ADULTERATE *OR* HANDLE DISHONESTLY THE WORD OF GOD, BUT WE STATE THE TRUTH OPENLY (CLEARLY AND CANDIDLY). AND SO WE COMMEND OURSELVES IN THE SIGHT *AND* PRESENCE OF GOD TO EVERY MAN'S CONSCIENCE.
(2 CORINTHIANS 4:2)

READING: PROVERBS 6:16-20

THE other day, I got a phone call from a woman who, at one point in time, was very involved with the ministry. She was always available and was good about giving and covering what was needed. She wanted to be in ministry. We took care of her ordination and set her on a proper path to achieve her goals. Not long after she was ordained, she decided she wanted to get a job. There's nothing wrong with this of course, because we all have different financial situations, and sometimes going to work is necessary. Something happened to her after she went to work, however. Work became her total focus, and she was no longer interested, nor a part of the ministry. No longer was she interested in giving, participating, or pursuing the work of the ministry available to her. She wanted to work and make money to purchase things for herself and her family, and the work of ministry became a distant memory.

On a few occasions over the past few years, we were in financial straits and needed those who were a part of the ministry to help. It is a given that being a part of the ministry requires tithing, but it is often difficult to get people to cooperate. No matter how hard I would try, this particular woman, who was making good money, wasn't willing to give. On the few occasions she was willing to do so, the money either never showed up, or she would forget to send it. As time went on, she was fired from her job and she appeared to be repentant for her actions, but she did nothing to make them right. It was the same old story, over again, promising to give or to purchase items, that never came to pass.

This woman is just one example of the many encounters I've had with dishonesty over time. The problem of dishonesty has become so common in the past few years, it has become near epidemic. We don't think twice about living in a manner that fails to be truthful and to answer for that covert lifestyle. When people are dishonest, it is a lifestyle of accountability avoidance. When confronted, there is always a reason why they didn't do something, but they never make the situation right or try to rectify things. Instead, they use their dishonesty to explain their dishonesty and avoid the truth and realities of dishonesty at all costs.

Dishonesty is a form of lying, because it operates with the intent to deceive. We don't think about it that way, but whenever we attempt to be dishonest with someone else, we are trying to manipulate a situation to our advantage so we can avoid doing the right thing. The right thing is not always the easy thing. Much of the time, the right thing costs us something, and I am not talking about money. It costs us growth and sacrifice, something we like to avoid. We don't want to feel pain or the strain of growth, and nobody likes the idea of having to sacrifice. But we can't claim to be Christian and claim to be people of faith if we don't want to give, and we want to cover that fact up. Whenever we feel we need to hide something, cover something up, or attempt to worm out of it, odds are good we are doing something dishonestly, hoping to avoid accountability and personal growth from it.

The longer you hold to dishonesty, the longer you will stay right where you are. You can't grow without giving; you can't excel without sacrifice; and you can't become all you desire to be if God can't break through your dishonest heart.

- DAY 69 -
Pruning

ANY BRANCH IN ME THAT DOES NOT BEAR FRUIT [THAT STOPS BEARING] HE CUTS AWAY (TRIMS OFF, TAKES AWAY); AND HE CLEANSES *AND* REPEATEDLY PRUNES EVERY BRANCH THAT CONTINUES TO BEAR FRUIT, TO MAKE IT BEAR MORE *AND* RICHER *AND* MORE EXCELLENT FRUIT.
(JOHN 15:2)

READING: ISAIAH 18:1-7

PRUNING is a popular topic in Christian circles. Part of why we like to discuss it is because we like to seek any reason to cut people out of our lives that we don't like. If we do it in the name of "pruning," we can get rid of anyone who irks us or rubs us the wrong way. It sounds good to call it "pruning" because it makes our fleshly virtue of holding grudges and animosity seem spiritual. Call it whatever we will, there's nothing spiritual about making the decision to remove people from our lives because we don't like them. Pruning is a different process that is spiritual in nature, and having to come face-to-face with it in my own life in the past couple of years has made me see exactly why the Bible talks about it as a hard process.

"Pruning" is not so much an adventure in eliminating people from one's life as it is from removing anything from one's life that causes them hindrance in the things of God. Sometimes this may take the form of people, but it can also come through habits, issues, attitudes, the way we spend our time, or our personal lack of focus. It's easy for us to think we have it all together and are more advanced than we really are, and pruning is a process that reveals exactly where we are. When we take away all our excesses, fanfare, fanciness and flora and fauna that disguise and cover the bareness of our realities, we need to have strong grounding, bases, roots and stem structures to come back, year after year during periods of silence and rest.

When I started this season, I had many people around me. Some I thought of as friends, and many were associates in ministry or were part of our ministry under my leadership. They seemed interested and happy, and acted as if they really had my back. As one by one most of them started to fade away, the question became, how was I going to make it? I had grown so used to their encouragement, prayers (or what I thought were prayers), ideas and support, I was not sure what could become of me or the work without them.

Those people had to go — they had to be pruned — because I was relying on them too much for the success and future of our ministry. It's easy to get used to certain people and patterns of behavior, especially when those are things that seem to be good or positive in your life. We think they'll all be there forever, and when pruning begins, it's a real adjustment to find life without them.

Whenever our spiritual lives are dictated by other people, those people have become idols in our lives that weaken our spiritual position with God. More often than not, genuine pruning doesn't come about with people who seek to do us harm or we don't like, but people and habits we do like, things that help us to function and keep going. They are the people and things we've learned to rely on, because they help us "bloom" and thrive, showing ourselves off to the world. They help us be someone and something in the eyes of others, no matter where we are with God ourselves.

Pruning shows us what is really there — or not — in our spiritual lives. When we are pruned, everything is removed that has eye appeal to outsiders. The results don't look pretty, we don't feel good about ourselves or where we are heading, and we don't desire to show off to the world. In times of pruning, we see our needed change, draw on divine strength, and look to none but God to make us bloom once again.

- DAY 70 -
Just Because I Don't Say Anything Doesn't Mean I Don't Know What's Going on

SO BE DONE WITH EVERY TRACE OF WICKEDNESS (DEPRAVITY, MALIGNITY) AND ALL DECEIT AND INSINCERITY (PRETENSE, HYPOCRISY) AND GRUDGES (ENVY, JEALOUSY) AND SLANDER *AND* EVIL SPEAKING OF EVERY KIND.
(1 PETER 2:1)

READING: 1 PETER 2:12-17

WHEN I was a kid, "Just because I don't say anything doesn't mean I don't know what's going on!" were my mother's hallowed words. In all fairness, my mother was not the type of parent who gave away all she knew. She liked to sit back and watch us and then stun us with her amazing and fanciful wealth of knowledge that proved she was no punk. When I was little, however, I didn't appreciate the wisdom in her statement. I felt like it meant she wasn't getting involved and was just trying to force us to work things out. I was half-right: she was giving us the space and time needed to try and work out our own situations. She gave us the time we needed to do the right thing and problem solve without adult interference, because she knew we would one day be adults and would have to do things ourselves. It wouldn't have taught us anything to run in and referee every single thing that came up in our lives. If we needed something or things got out of control, she would be there, but overall, we needed to learn how to work things out ourselves.

As a leader, I used to be overly involved with the people I cover, and sometimes even with my friends. I was fast to be there for them any time something came up, and I would get right in and get involved. I would do this, even in disagreements between people. For example, if someone came to talk with me about what another did, I would immediately take sides. I did this because I felt I knew the character of the individual who came and told me the story, and that was enough to go by to take a stand against the other person they were talking about. I wound up in a complete and total mess, more than once. Being in the middle of things between people is never easy and leads to a lot of hard feelings and offenses with others. When the other side retaliated, I retaliated back, and so on and so forth. It became a loud, wild, unspeakable mess, and I got involved in it because I didn't have the good sense to stay out of it.

When "Just because I don't say anything doesn't mean I don't know what's going on!" came out of my mouth a few years ago. It surprised me. It wasn't one of those "I'm becoming my mother" moments; it was because that was not an expression I ever expected to say, or see the value in, in my own life. It came about because I had enough experience of getting involved where I shouldn't to know most situations aren't as simple as people make them out to be. As people, we love to look like the victim, like we've been wronged, and it's not uncommon to find people telling a lot of half-truths to make sure you will side with them when the time comes. Sitting back and having knowledge of what is going on is never bad, because it affords the opportunity to remain objective and uninvolved in situations. In most settings like this, there needs to be a voice of objective reason, one that can help one or both parties find themselves and their heads and make the decision to be civil or disassociate. The more people who deliberately involve themselves, the more out of control and unreasonable all involved become.

It's great and fine to be someone that others trust as a confidant, but being a confidant doesn't mean taking sides in any given situation. Know what's going on, keep opinions to yourself, and give others the time and ability to sort things out for themselves.

- Day 71 -
I Wish You Were Here

Now the Lord God said, It is not good (sufficient, satisfactory) that the man should be alone; I will make him a helper (suitable, adapted, complementary) for him.
(Genesis 2:18)

Reading: Psalm 25:16-22

As a general statement, I am not a lonely person. I like having space and quiet to sort through thoughts and concepts. In ministry, I spend a lot of time having to attend to different needs, and some of those needs take a distinctly parental form, so I am grateful for the times I do not have to take care of anyone. I always have lots to do, so projects fill a lot of space that might otherwise be spent idle. Still, from time to time I will go through periods of intense loneliness. I'm blessed it's not something that happens often. When it does, I am sure it's not hard to imagine just why it comes up. It's been said, the higher we go, the fewer the people who surround us, and that is definitely something I have experienced. The more I seek to be serious about the things of God, I find fewer people understand where I am coming from. This changes our relationship interactions. When any one of us feels misunderstood, it can cause us to feel alone. While it's easy to tell others that we don't need people in our lives who no longer serve a purpose, it's a lot harder to be the person who lives with those results.

Yes, we have God, and I would hope you'd know that I understand that. I also recognize even God Himself didn't set Himself against human companionship. Back in the garden,

Adam had God and all the animals, and God recognized it wasn't enough. He needed a living, breathing person there to not only stand as a companion, but also challenge and compliment him in different ways. Having another person around was a part of human experience, and it's no different with us today. Trying to substitute God for human companionship is always a bad idea, not super-spiritual and deep. The more we grow in God, we understand not everyone is always there like we might like, but we also recognize the important role and position God plays in our lives.

Loneliness is an awful thing to experience, but I believe it serves a purpose in our lives if we will only look past the emotion and hurt to see the message behind it. When we are lonely, it's a sign we have outgrown what we have and who we have in the immediacy of our lives. It's a signpost of spiritual growth, one of a new chapter and a new beginning. (As much as we cheerlead new beginnings, our dislike of loneliness proves otherwise.) The void we feel means something new is there to take its place, something ready for the horizon that we haven't yet experienced. Gaps are hard, but not nearly as hard as staying somewhere far beyond their useful time.

As I have seen many come and go in this season, I have experienced lonely periods. Experiencing it can mess with your better judgment, and I've had plenty of days where I wondered if maybe I did the wrong thing or should try to do something to change the situations as they were. When the moments lifted, I realized the negative feelings of loneliness were just that: moments. As with all moments, they pass, they lift to reveal something else, and I started seeing my world in a new way. Those who were in my life already or in it for the first time had new purposes, I had new things to do, and those who had left weren't so important anymore.

When we get lonely, all we want is that void to be filled. Instead of randomly filling voids with wrong things, we need to wait throughout the period to see those in our lives clearer and more defined. Embracing change always brings new possibilities to us.

- Day 72 -
Our Father Who art in Heaven

A FATHER OF THE FATHERLESS AND A JUDGE *AND* PROTECTOR OF THE WIDOWS *IS* GOD
IN HIS HOLY HABITATION. GOD PLACES THE SOLITARY IN FAMILIES *AND* GIVES THE DESOLATE
A HOME IN WHICH TO DWELL; HE LEADS THE PRISONERS OUT TO PROSPERITY; BUT THE
REBELLIOUS DWELL IN A PARCHED LAND.
(PSALM 68:5-6)

READING: MATTHEW 12:46-50

IT'S not a big secret to say I don't have the best relationship with my biological father. It's probably more accurate to say I don't have any relationship with him. It's a long, drawn-out story that extends from childhood to the present day, and it's not pretty. He and I were antagonistic from the day I was born, and that made for some interesting childhood memories. They were not all bad, not by a longshot (nothing is seldom all good or all bad), but there wasn't enough good to outweigh the bad. My parents separated when I was seven. From that point on, I had little involvement with him in life. There were a few years of visits, but that was it. He was so awful to be around, I didn't want to be with him. Except for a few incidents that were less than ideal, I haven't had any connection with him in many years.

Being a child of divorce and being a child without an active father is often considered a fate worse than death in many Christian circles. People automatically assume you have all sorts of problems and are incapable of substantial relationships. They assume you must have deep-seated hurts life that require a specified "healing" before you can do anything with your life. Maybe the worst thing for me was it often meant people questioned my leadership or personality. They would brand me in a specific light because they didn't like something about me, and that meant there must be something wrong with me. More than once, it resulted in bullying and commands to "rectify" things when such a command was not even sensibly Biblical. It made me feel as if there was something about me that would forever be wrong, even if I felt fine and felt that what they were saying was both unfounded and in error.

I didn't have a chronic loss of "fatherlessness." I had the problem of being judged and trying to meet up with the expectations others had for me. I had an unfortunate run-in with people who were trying to be someone at the expense of my own spiritual well-being and personal feelings. It wasn't until a few months ago that I heard some words that completely changed my perspective: "It's not your experience." Uttered by Dr. Phil during one of his shows, those four words changed the way I felt about every person who came and tried to "fix" what was not broken in me in my adult life. No, I don't have the childhood memories of being my "father's daughter" or of feeling safe and comfortable with my biological father. I am not, however, and have never, ever been "fatherless." If we know God as our Father and we truly believe He is our Father, there is no such thing as "fatherlessness." We might not have an earthly parent to speak of, but our heavenly parent is forever there, ready to transform us and give us the best life possible, regardless of what is or is not our experience.

When it comes to absentee or deceased parents, we all should be more cautious of how we speak to others about such things. Loss of a parent isn't a new thing. For thousands of years, parents have been lost due to war, famine, illness, abandonment, divorce or separation, immigration, and so many more things that happen during life and living. Such doesn't make the children involve damaged goods, incapable of relationships, or of being who God called them to be. Yes, not having a parent can be hard, but it gets a lot easier when we know our heavenly Father will be there for us through eternity.

- Day 73 -
Hope Deferred

WHY ARE YOU CAST DOWN, O MY INNER SELF? AND WHY SHOULD YOU MOAN OVER ME *AND* BE DISQUIETED WITHIN ME? HOPE IN GOD *AND* WAIT EXPECTANTLY FOR HIM, FOR I SHALL YET PRAISE HIM, MY HELP AND MY GOD.
(PSALM 42:5)

READING: JEREMIAH 29:10-14

I'VE wanted a pair of Irregular Choice shoes for as long as I can remember. I've never bought a pair because they always seemed so expensive. Sure, they are nowhere near what a pair of Louboutins or Gucci shoes cost, but to me, my shoe cutoff is somewhere around $75. I have a few pairs that cost more than that, but very, very few. Especially given my financial constraints the past few years, I'm not apt to spend money on shoes like I once did. There are tons of knockoffs that look just like the real thing that are under $50, so there's no reason to go out of my way and spend so much more than is necessary. So, when a pair of Irregular Choice came across my feed, I wanted to consider them, but they seemed like so much money. A woman I know suggested going to Burlington Coat Factory, as she used to find the brand there when she would frequent a store in Massachusetts.

I figured it was worth a try, even if it was a longshot. I assumed it had been a few years since she had seen them there, but Burlington Coat Factory is always nice to walk through and explore. One lazy Saturday afternoon that followed a busy Saturday morning, I decided it was time to venture out, so my mom and I decided to make a "little trip" out to the Burlington Coat Factory, about ten minutes from my apartment. The trip seemed simple enough. It was an easy drive, and when we pulled up to the small strip mall, things felt...eerie. For one, all the shops at that end of the mall were either closed or had no one on active duty. In one store, the saleswoman said she would be right out and left us standing there for ten minutes. In another, it clearly said the store was open until 9 PM (it was only about 4 PM), and all their doors were locked. Maybe the most poignant piece of evidence was the closed, sealed metal door to the Burlington Coat Factory entrance. It had been closed for so long, there was a bench in front of it. We started trying to defer all sorts of ideas as to why this might be: maybe that entrance was closed off, maybe they closed early, or the one I came up with...maybe the store was closed. There had never been any announcement of the store closing or a clearance sale. I know that with good assurance, because I would have heard and gone to the final sales. As we walked around to the front of the building, we stood in front of a completely empty store. There was nothing, and I repeat nothing, in there: no shelves, light fixtures, no registers, no leftover merchandise...nothing. It was a lost picture of what used to be there.

My hope of obtaining a pair of Irregular Choice shoes from Burlington Coat Factory was no more. If I wanted a pair, I was going to have to find an affordable one online, and let it go at that. My hope might have drained in that moment, but it was truly a moment where it was nothing more than deferred. I knew I would find a pair of my desired Irregular Choice shoes, and that promise was not lost because they didn't have a Burlington Coat Factory where one used to stand.

Sometimes our hope is deferred for things much bigger and more relevant than a great pair of shoes. We might look out over our situations and our feelings about things and wonder if they will ever be different. If you are where you are supposed to be in the right time, hope is only deferred. Hold on to the promise in a great pair of shoes and don't let a sense of delay get you into a bad place long-term.

- DAY 74 -
Gossip, Gossip, Gossip!

YOU SHALL NOT REPEAT *OR* RAISE A FALSE REPORT; YOU SHALL NOT JOIN WITH THE WICKED
TO BE AN UNRIGHTEOUS WITNESS.
(EXODUS 23:1)

READING: JAMES 1:23-27

A couple of years back, a woman in an organization I was once part of set her sights to spread stories and rumors about another woman in the organization. When she came to me with her story, I was angry about it. It wasn't a story that was really believable. I was annoyed that she wasted my time with such a ridiculous thing. It wasn't a story that, even if it was true, I could do anything about, so I was really annoyed that she forced me to take time to consider how to handle the situation. The one thing I made sure to happen was the story died with me. I was not going to run to half the organization with it and spread the story any further, because it needed to die. When she didn't get what she wanted with me, she went and told the story to someone else who didn't respond the way she wanted, and then took it to someone else, who finally bit the way she'd hoped. The story then spread like wildfire through several members of the group, because both women were unable to keep the story to themselves. When push came to shove, they wanted to share the tidbit they discovered, all for different reasons. One wanted to spread malicious stories, while the other wanted to expound on her personal ideas about handling the issue at hand. It turned into a gigantic mess, one where feelings were hurt, people wound up offended, and many wound up not speaking to each other any longer. It was a tragic scene that served as a powerful reminder of the negative force gossip can become.

Gossip is a part of our lives. It is something every single one of us has done at some point in time. We've all spread a story, maybe unwittingly, about someone else, that has gone from channel to channel. Maybe it was in the name of praying for them, and you just let a little too much information slip. Maybe it wasn't quite so altruistic, and you were eager to give more information than you should about someone else, because you were angry with them or wanted to get back at them for something. Still, gossip has a way of slipping into the ordinary conversation in the name of fitting in, having something to talk about, or just wanting to fill an awkward moment with something, anything, that shifts the focus away from you and any mishaps or *faux pas* incurred since the last conversation.

I'm making a point not to be too preachy about gossip, because we all know the Scriptures give heavy warnings against it. Gossip has the potential to ruin friendships and relationships, nowadays with the advance of social media, it can damage people's careers or affect their jobs, and it has been known to severely hurt families. If you've ever been the victim of gossip, you know these statements are not an exaggeration, in the least. The very minimal damage of gossip comes in the form of direct offense between parties, and that is definitely enough damage to keep in mind and consider the ramifications of such behavior.

If we understand the Christian life in the light of service and love of others, gossip isn't a viable option for us. We are supposed to love and care for others, not spread crazy stories about them. True or not, firsthand or not, things said in confidence need to remain in confidence. If we want to be people that others desire to talk to, love, and trust, we need to exemplify the functions of trustworthiness in our own lives and walk. Gossip might seem fun and connecting for the moment, but when someone winds up hurt, it's obvious the price is higher than it's worth.

- Day 75 -
Meeting the Spirit Again for the Very First Time

BUT WHEN HE, THE SPIRIT OF TRUTH (THE TRUTH-GIVING SPIRIT) COMES, HE WILL GUIDE YOU INTO ALL THE TRUTH (THE WHOLE, FULL TRUTH). FOR HE WILL NOT SPEAK HIS OWN MESSAGE [ON HIS OWN AUTHORITY]; BUT HE WILL TELL WHATEVER HE HEARS [FROM THE FATHER; HE WILL GIVE THE MESSAGE THAT HAS BEEN GIVEN TO HIM], AND HE WILL ANNOUNCE *AND* DECLARE TO YOU THE THINGS THAT ARE TO COME [THAT WILL HAPPEN IN THE FUTURE].
(JOHN 16:13)

READING: ACTS 1:1-8

I'M not new to the realm of spiritual activity in the life of a believer. I know that there are still many people who are unfamiliar with the way the Spirit can work in an everyday context, but I haven't considered myself to be one of those people in a very long time. I'm not a Spirit-denier, but I was one who commonly associated my understanding of the Spirit with what I was told it was in church. In most churches that identify themselves as "Spirit-filled," activity identified with the Spirit is assumed to be loud and exuberant. The louder the praise, the more "Spirit-filled" it is assumed to be. Those who experience the power of the Spirit may fall, shake, dance, run around, yell, or experience any other number of deliverance experiences that are also dramatic and notable in their observance. This has led to several people who think this is the only way the Spirit can show up and show out in a church service.

I grew up in a traditional church that was very quiet. We weren't allowed to make noise. As a result, this extreme opposite of spiritual activity was notably more attractive to me (especially in the early years). It seemed so much more energetic, and you could feel how excited those at the church were about God. It made my church of origin pale in comparison, and seemed like a dull, dry, dead experience that would turn anyone off. How could God be in a place that seemed so dead, and how could God not be in a place where people were so excited and welcoming to the work of the Spirit?

What I have come to see now is the contrast in extremes. I have seen the results of both extremes over the years, and the result is the same. In my church of origin, people were spiritually dead and lacking, because there was obviously nothing of substance there to give them the boost and purpose in their everyday lives. They didn't know God was someone to be experienced through the Spirit, and they never had the opportunity to be excited about what He could do for them. On the contrast, always feeling the need to kick up, louder and louder, and assume that is always the Spirit leads to the same sense of ritual and tradition; they are just different rituals and traditions. It's possible to scream, shout, run around the church, talk about how awesome church was and believe God can do anything and still be dead inside, performing exterior motions that are louder than others, but equally lead to nowhere. No matter how enthusiastic someone might be on the outside, they can still be dead on the inside.

Through this time in my life, I have started to come to a place of balance on matters of the Spirit. The Spirit doesn't always move through a room and shut the place down, but God is always present with us, whether we feel exuberant, or not. Part of the call of the Christian life is to discover this divine presence, guiding and leading us on, even if we don't understand everything about it or "feel" it in the way we have been led to believe it is there. The Scriptures teach us the Holy Spirit exists to lead us into all truth, comfort us, and breathe life and purpose into the church, and He does this by working through each one of us as we are willing to allow Him to work within and through us in all things. No, every day won't be a rocking church service, and it doesn't have to be void and dead, either, but if we call ourselves Christians, we should know and recognize the Spirit is always there.

- Day 76 -
My Name is no!

AND YOU SHALL SET BOUNDS FOR THE PEOPLE ROUND ABOUT, SAYING, TAKE HEED THAT YOU GO NOT UP INTO THE MOUNTAIN OR TOUCH THE BORDER OF IT. WHOEVER TOUCHES THE MOUNTAIN SHALL SURELY BE PUT TO DEATH. NO HAND SHALL TOUCH IT [OR THE OFFENDER], BUT HE SHALL SURELY BE STONED OR SHOT [WITH ARROWS]; WHETHER BEAST OR MAN, HE SHALL NOT LIVE. WHEN THE TRUMPET SOUNDS A LONG BLAST, THEY SHALL COME UP TO THE MOUNTAIN.
(EXODUS 19:12-13)

READING: DEUTERONOMY 19:1-14

I'VE discovered the most empowering word ever invented. It's not a particularly popular word. Most people have trouble spitting it out and concede every time. That word is no.

I am officially in love with the word "no." It's never been a word I have feared, and it is certainly a word I've heard often enough in my many years of ministry. Regardless, "no" was a word I learned to avoid. It was implied (and sometimes stated outright) that saying "no" to people would lead to bad things in ministry: a reputation for being difficult, acting out in offense, being selfish, or being disagreeable. It's silently understood that telling people no, or insisting they are not behaving properly around you so you won't have it, is going to make sure you never have any people in your ministry, your ministry will not grow, and you will be left out of conferences and other events, because people won't like you.

These not-so-subtle pressures extend into every minister's psyche with vengeance. It's natural for us to want to succeed in the ministry and do whatever we are called to do to the best of our ability. If going above and beyond is what it will take, then most of us are willing to do that. I was no different. It didn't help that every time I said no to someone or tried to set up boundaries, the inevitable happened. Just as is implied, my boundaries became the very excuse those people used to justify the reasons why they didn't include me in things or desire to remain a part of the work. Then, one day, I figured out the truth behind the veneer: it was an excuse. When push came to shove, they weren't going to have me out, or participate anyway, so they would just use the fact that I set a boundary as their reasoning, even though the decision had already been made.

I know this was the case, because there are scores of people I did not say no to who used this ministry, the abilities I have, and the work, some for years, and the results were the same. We live in a church world that's itching to have its own way, and the competition therein makes it so we assess others by their ability to make us look good or present the way we hope to present. Saying no is taboo, because we don't respect each other in the way we should to promote proper ministry growth and forward movement.

Over the past year, God has put me in several positions to get real comfortable telling people no, and there is something empowering about it. By saying no, I am establishing self-respect. I am respecting the gifts God has placed within me. I am reminded that everything God wants to do within this ministry merits the respect of other people. My time is valuable, my experience is valuable, and I am valuable. This isn't about the right price or doing things for money; it is about recognizing not everyone and everything out there has our best interests at heart, and the sooner we discern who that is from who it is not, we will be more successful in the ministry.

Saying no may mean some people never talk to you again, or it might mean they will try again. It means you find out who is really riding with you and who is for you, and who isn't. Ministry is about relationships and connection, and the only way we find out who is right and who is wrong is through that dreaded little word: no.

- DAY 77 -
Learning About Faith Again and Again

So shall My word be that goes forth out of My mouth: it shall not return to Me void [without producing any effect, useless], but it shall accomplish that which I please *and* purpose, and it shall prosper in the thing for which I sent it.
(Isaiah 55:11)

READING: HEBREWS 11:1-13

WHEN Sanctuary International Fellowship Tabernacle – SIFT started out in its first building, things were very different than they wound up being a year or so later. In the first place, we were Sanctuary Apostolic Fellowship. What we were doing was so new, I wasn't always sure what to do or how to do it. It wasn't my first church experience, but it was my first experience in a new time, with a new vision and (what I believed was) a new season. I was working with a new demographic group of people, and it was my first personal church establishment in the southeast. We'd previously had ministry offices, and I covered leaders who had their own ministries, but starting and handling it myself was an entirely different thing, especially from week to week. It was the first time we were in a building I had to pay for, and I knew from the outset, meeting it monthly would be a challenge. Because God was in this, however, I trusted that the money would be there.

Things started out promising. About eight weeks into the lease, God revealed to me that we wouldn't finish out the lease. The reason we would leave the building would have nothing to do with non-payment. This was a relief to me, but God didn't specify why we would be leaving the building. So, me and my big ego decided we'd be leaving because we would outgrow the place before the lease was up. We had a family attending and people in different locations who promised to visit and support the work, so I assumed the small building we had would become too tiny, and moving would be in order. This assumption of mine jazzed me up for whatever was to come.

The problem was this scenario of mine wasn't what happened. Over time, the family that was excited and ready for anything started to lose interest and stopped coming regularly. They were in and out, sometimes with the kids and sometimes not, and most of our proclaimed visitors didn't show up. Somehow, the rent was paid every month, we reached many people far and wide with our videos, and a whole new group of people were interested in what we were doing. We had some other people in and out of the church; guests who came every so often when they could, and others who liked what we were doing, even if they only came once or twice. We even had an ordination ceremony before leaving the property. Just as God promised, every need was met, even in seasons where it didn't seem as if it would happen.

We were two months out before the end of the lease, and I just assumed I hadn't heard from God at that point in time. I was ready to be done with the property and prepare for whatever we were supposed to do next. We'd been complaining about a leak in the roof that was seeping through the walls for some time, but it came to our attention that the building had a severe mold infestation. In a single weekend, we had to move out of the property – early, and not due to non-payment of rent. Suddenly, God's words to me came flooding back. We had to leave, we were moving out, and it had nothing to do with our finances. God's word was true.

No matter how advanced we are or how great our calling may seem to us, we can all use a crash-course reminder in the relevance of faith in our lives and in trusting in God. Filling in the blanks is too common when God doesn't tell us the whole story, but those are the very situations faith is for. As we learn faith, we learn God, and His ways, again and again...just a little deeper, each time.

- Day 78 -
Grace-Full

> And he came to her and said, Hail, O favored one [endued with grace]!
> The Lord is with you! Blessed (favored of God) are you before all other women!
> But *when she saw him*, she was greatly troubled *and* disturbed
> *and* confused at what he said and kept revolving in her mind what such
> a greeting might mean. And the angel said to her, Do not be afraid, Mary,
> for you have found grace (free, spontaneous, absolute favor and loving-
> kindness) with God.
> (Luke 1:28-30)

Reading: Luke 1:39-55

MARY was the first Bible woman I ever studied with the goal to learn anything about her. I learned about her before Eve, before Deborah, before Bathsheba, before Mary Magdalene, and before any of the other women, anywhere in the Bible. When I was in junior high, I completed a religious Girl Scout program to receive what is called the "Marian Medal." In process, I had to learn about Mary's life and what she experienced as a human being, a woman in the first century. Seeing Mary as a person was new for me, because Mary was a central figure in the church where I grew up. We didn't treat her as if she was a person, though. She was more than just a human being in that church; she took on the nature of a female goddess. She was so central, she was idolized and worshipped to a point where we didn't know what was true or what wasn't about her. We didn't treat Mary as if she had any personage at all, but was a strange, mystical figure whose life had no ordinary characteristics from her literal conception. When I had to read about Mary as a person, it was a shock for me. All of a sudden, she became...real. She was someone who could have been you, me, or anyone else around us, who became the mother of Jesus Christ. She wasn't fancy. She wasn't extraordinary. She was nobody and nothing from nowhere who became something incredible, because God knew her humility and ordinary heart would prompt her to great obedience.

I recorded a program for *Power For Today* last year that was all about Mary, prompting me to look at her again. This wasn't the first time I studied Mary or her life since that project I did years ago. Every so many years, Mary and her life come up again somehow, some way, and I wind up teaching on her and her life. There was something different I noticed when I recorded the teaching this time, however. For the first time, I considered the concept of Mary as "full of grace." That was something I'd never considered in all the years I'd studied and taught on Mary and her experience. To become the mother of Jesus and conceive of the Holy Spirit, she had to become full of grace, so full of grace that there was room for nothing else within her. I don't know if that is a concept we can conceive, because whenever people try to go that route in Mary's experience, the tendency is to look at her. Surely an ordinary person can't be full of grace, so we must make her something else. Conceived without sin, perhaps? Destined for ministry from the time she was four? A Levite? All these teachings started somewhere, but they completely ignore the concept of grace in the life and work of Mary. By proxy, they also ignore it within us.

Mary was full of grace – she was "grace-full." She was so full of the love and purpose of God's divine favor that echoed how good God was, there wasn't room for anything else in her. Her experience as being full of grace echoed into her relationship with God, because she trusted Him. Because she was so full of grace, Mary was able to birth something amazing and supernatural with God. It's no different for us. Mary wasn't born without sin or set apart as a child; she was just a person who knew her God and what He could do. Being full of grace left no room for the earthly fears and anxieties she might later experience, as it led her to proclaim whatever was God's will, she was ready for it. God can do the same work within us, if we will but trust Him, and leave no room for anything but His amazing grace within us.

- Day 79 -
Going First

> Issachar's host as numbered totaled 54,400. Then the tribe of Zebulun,
> Eliab son of Helon being the leader of the sons of Zebulun. Zebulun's host
> as numbered totaled 57,400. All these [three tribes] numbered in the camp
> of Judah totaled 186,400. They shall set forth first [on the march].
> (Numbers 2:6-9)

Reading: 2 Corinthians 8:1-8

I've often discussed the concept of the apostolic office as one where we are supposed to "go first." The early apostles were the first ones in new lands, territories, and spiritual grounds to proclaim the presence of the Kingdom of God. Those who follow in the footsteps of those early apostles are here to do the same: go first and proclaim the Kingdom of God. The way we may be called to do it might not take the exact same form, but going first is a key aspect of the apostolic. We are supposed to be those who are not afraid to go out and bring needed change, to do things that have never been done before, and to be the first in any place to do what needs doing.

Two years ago, I went to preach for a conference in Daytona Beach, Florida. I didn't know the pastor who invited me and I didn't handle most of the arrangements (I had an assistant at the time). When I arrived at the hotel and met the church's pastor, I had never seen him before, and he had never seen me before in person. As we sat down to dine at a restaurant, he looked at me and said, "Let's get this out of the way – you are the first white woman to ever preach in my church. Actually, you are the first white person to ever preach in my church, period." I looked at him and replied, "I'm the first white person to preach in a lot of places. This isn't my first time." That was a true statement. There are churches I have preached in up and down the east coast, especially in the deep south, where no Caucasian man or woman darkened the doorway throughout their history, and none has since. It has never bothered nor phased me, because that is a part of my apostolic work. I am here, as I am, to go first.

People often think going first is a glory job, but it's not. It means being in a lot of situations that get you a lot of stares and make people wonder what you are doing there. It means not everyone receives you in the way you might like, and some treat you with suspicion. Being first means nobody like you has ever been there before, and it may be a while before someone else like you comes along, after. Being first means being prepared, ready for anything and everything that comes your way. It takes preparation, honest examination, and a deconstruction of everything within you that wants your own way and to stay away from others. In going first, I must confront my fears, my insecurities, and the things that keep me away from my true destiny.

We seldom discuss the level of personal sacrifice it takes to be in the ministry. It might not be pretty, but it is an essential aspect of this work that we don't deal with enough. Being in ministry means those of us who are called to leadership gain their needed spiritual insight and growth as leaders in the church. Our place, our needed development, and our experience with God is a part of our leadership. If we don't stretch ourselves, we will never burn up the spiritual dross within us so gold can come forth and God can work both within and through us within His plan.

Somebody must go first; it might as well be me. It might as well be each and every apostle God has duly called in this time to do something different, be something more, step out and challenge, change, and do what needs doing. There is a whole world out there of needed firsts, experiences, and leaders who need to walk as God has called them so we can build the Kingdom of God together.

- Day 80 -
This is Who I Am

WELCOME *AND* RECEIVE [TO YOUR HEARTS] ONE ANOTHER, THEN, EVEN AS CHRIST
HAS WELCOMED *AND* RECEIVED YOU, FOR THE GLORY OF GOD. FOR I TELL YOU THAT CHRIST
(THE MESSIAH) BECAME A SERVANT *AND* A MINISTER TO THE CIRCUMCISED (THE JEWS)
IN ORDER TO SHOW GOD'S TRUTHFULNESS *AND* HONESTY BY CONFIRMING (VERIFYING)
THE PROMISES [GIVEN] TO OUR FATHERS, AND [ALSO IN ORDER] THAT THE GENTILES
(NATIONS) MIGHT GLORIFY GOD FOR HIS MERCY [NOT COVENANTED] TO THEM. AS IT IS
WRITTEN, THEREFORE I WILL PRAISE YOU AMONG THE GENTILES AND SING PRAISES
TO YOUR NAME.
(ROMANS 15:7-9)

READING: COLOSSIANS 3:9-15

My name is Lee Ann, and I have a confession to make: I hate sitting on the pulpit platform. Yes, I know I am a minister and a preacher, and I am supposed to love it up there, but I hate it up there. I've tried; I really have. It's just not my thing. I feel disconnected from the congregation, like I am on display. I want to sit in the back, where nobody knows who I am and see how they treat me. I think that's a better test of character and integrity, don't you agree? Not to mention, I am just not in love with the idea of being so visible up there. You can't sneeze, go to the bathroom, or do anything without everyone seeing you.

While I am in a confessing mood, I have another one: I am not into robes and collars. In fact, I like them about as much as I like sitting on the pulpit platform, which is not at all. Collars are tight, they look like a dog collar on me, and I have yet to find a collar and shirt that fits me properly. Robes are heavy, hot, and too long. Cleaning them is a nightmare. They are expensive. Let's be real, they are also ugly. I have lovely clothes that fit me properly, and I am just as anointed in my own clothes as I am in something else, so I prefer to wear my own clothes. I have the formal wear for formal occasions...but those are the only times they crawl out of the closet. The rest of the time, they stay in there under something else I would rather wear.

Last confession: I do not accept the "chief apostle" label. Many use it to express their supremacy over an organization, but all I hear is the Apostle Paul throwing spiritual shade at stupid, arrogant people who were into themselves. I don't do "chief," "master," "major," or any of that mess. No one covered by me is allowed to embrace such mess within their own organizations. We don't do ridiculous, expensive, over-the-top ceremonies. We are about that which is Biblical, upholding ministry as it is found therein in our modern context, and we leave it at that.

None of these things are what makes or breaks a ministry, or at least, they shouldn't. Being in ministry shouldn't be about the outfits we wear, where we sit in a church, or the expansive titles we call ourselves. Yet, somehow, these things have come to define so much of who and what ministers are, we have lost sight of what we are really called to do and who we are called to be. I don't think a minister is leading anyone to hell if they believe in such things, but I also can't jump on board with them and embrace them myself. Just as I don't expect everyone in the entire world to embrace my viewpoint, the same should be true in reverse. I shouldn't be deliberately left out because I don't want to wear a shirt and collar to preach every week or because I refuse to add superlatives to my name. My ministry and my work should speak for themselves, and I should be embraced for who I am rather than who I might appear to be in a specific outfit.

I've tried hard over the years to fit in, in ways and places that were neither purposeful, nor becoming to who I really am called to be. I even trained and considered being ordained as a bishop, which never wound up coming to pass. God wanted me to know myself, trust Him, and know that who He has created me to be is not only enough, but also needed in this time. I am who I am, and this is me. Take me or leave me, I'll be here when you're ready...just as I am.

- Day 81 -
Measures of Faith

For by the grace (unmerited favor of God) given to me I warn everyone among you not to estimate *and* think of himself more highly than he ought [not to have an exaggerated opinion of his own importance], but to rate his ability with sober judgment, each according to the degree of faith apportioned by God to him.
(Romans 12:3)

Reading: Matthew 25:14-30

WHEN Prophetess Theresa Bloodgood died in November of 2011, it wasn't a big surprise. She had been seriously ill with breast cancer for quite a while. Even before her cancer took a turn for the worst, she spent a few years in and out of chemotherapy and radiation treatment. The last few years of her life were spent in discomfort, nausea, and failing health. Regardless of this fact, she pulled herself together as best she could and set herself to minister. She would spend her days blogging, writing messages to her "spiritual children," as she called them, from all over the world. She was a decent teacher who expressed many reflections from her cancer experience in her work.

I knew Prophetess Bloodgood in a way some did not; I was her spiritual leader before she died. I helped prepare her for her prophet's ordination and worked closely with her in that time frame. Despite living in different states, we talked every day, most days for long periods of time. We shared about our lives, our ministries, our beliefs, and even tackled some current topics considering Christian teaching that proved very relevant later on in my ministry. I was her leader, teacher, and above all, she was my friend.

When I had the opportunity to speak about her and her work the other night, I was very excited. The longer someone is gone, the fewer opportunities come up to remember someone in shared conversation. The discussion took a turn I did not expect, however. The individual I was speaking to had known her in a specific context while she was sick, and in his mind's eye view, she didn't have enough "faith" to obey God. He expected that she would get on a plane while in treatment for breast cancer and assist him, however he needed it in Africa, during that process. Because she was unable to do that, he deemed her as having a lack of faith. When I tried to tell him that her situation rendered her unable to make that kind of step, but she still stepped out in faith and did what she was able to do, he wouldn't budge. His outlook was judgmental and relentless, and unflinching as he looked down upon a woman who spent most of her final years of life sick, in between appointments, and trying her best to maintain a good outlook. Was she perfect? Certainly not. She had issues, just like the rest of us do, but that doesn't mean she didn't have enough faith.

The Bible talks about each of us receiving a "measure of faith." This might sound strange if we talk about it in modern terms, but it proves God's purpose and work in our lives. God has given each of us a measure – or an amount – of faith that is plenty for whatever work it is we need to do. He has equipped us to tackle every mountain and take on every project that He starts and finishes within us. Before we were ever born, God knew what we would be able to do, what we would do, and how we can do it. Not all of us are destined to take on things in the Kingdom that others might do with ease. What is a big task for one of us might be nothing for someone else. It doesn't matter if what we do is measured by someone else; it only matters that in the sight of God, we are using the measure of faith we have.

To this very day, I miss my friend. Whenever something

happens, she is still the first person I want to tell, because her measure of faith was different from mine, but it was still enough. Her life reminds me to appreciate the different measures of faith that are around me, because therein lie each individuals' unique gifts and abilities.

- Day 82 -
The Kingdom of God is Within You!

AND WHEN HE WAS DEMANDED OF THE PHARISEES, WHEN THE KINGDOM OF GOD
SHOULD COME, HE ANSWERED THEM AND SAID, THE KINGDOM OF GOD COMETH NOT
WITH OBSERVATION: NEITHER SHALL THEY SAY, LO HERE! OR, LO THERE! FOR, BEHOLD,
THE KINGDOM OF GOD IS WITHIN YOU.
(LUKE 17:20-21, KJV)

READING: PSALM 145:1-15

WHEN I was a young believer, I came across a movie called *Stigmata*. I loved the way it showed the conflict between progress and change, new information and old ideals, and the way that tradition was accurately depicted as covering up so much reality we never hear about in connection with history. I also walked away from the movie with some limited information about the Gospel of Thomas, a document emerging in early Christianity that is a collection of sayings between Christ and His disciples. To me, it is not so much a question as to its veracity as much as it reveals the way people thought about Christ and His teachings in a time much closer to His life on earth than ours now, so that provides us important insights. My favorite aspect of the writing, however, is the true emphasis it places on the Kingdom. Kingdom-themed ideals have only come into vogue in the past decade or so but being Kingdom-focused and trained to see the Kingdom firsthand, up close and personal, and recognize the presence of God within us, even if it wasn't something we could see with the naked eye.

The past year or so, God has brought me back to my "Kingdom" themed roots. It wasn't something I taught on much for a while because the terminology has become so commonplace and cliché, I desired to avoid it. When you have only so many opportunities to preach, major themes sometimes get overshadowed in the name of something that speaks to those people, at that singular moment, right then and there. As I develop and things transform from one ministry passage to another, I realize the importance of the Kingdom, of understanding it in as foundational a way as the Gospel of Thomas speaks on it. We should come to a point where it is as near to us as something we can reach out and touch and something as normal as a function and discussion for our everyday lives. Kingdom should not be detached from us but should be us.

The Kingdom of God is a radical concept that we don't understand in our largely secular world today. By talking about the Kingdom of God in ancient times, believers were pitting themselves against the existing nations and powers that be. If Jesus was Lord, that meant Caesar (or fill in the blank for any name) was not. If believers hold to a different Kingdom, one that is out-of-this-world, that challenges their understanding and identity as citizens of any nation. It doesn't mean we cease to have rights where we are or that our nationalities change, but it does mean that our primary Kingdom understanding doesn't fall within the comfortable parameters of patriotism that we've grown accustomed to see in our modern days. Being a member of God's Kingdom means being something more than we can be if we rely on human identity alone to define us as people.

If we fail to understand the Kingdom of God within us, we will forever hold to traditions to identify us. Any time someone starts arguing about whether Christians can watch television, listen to music, watch movies, dance, or argue about attire, they don't understand the Kingdom of God within them. If we truly realize it is within us, then God is with us and a part of us no matter where we go or what we do. It doesn't mean anything goes, but it does mean the witness of the Spirit reminds us of our citizenship in all circumstances. Embracing this changes everything.

- Day 83 -
Rearranging

FOR THEN [CHANGING THEIR IMPURE LANGUAGE] I WILL GIVE TO THE PEOPLE A CLEAR
AND PURE SPEECH FROM PURE LIPS, THAT THEY MAY ALL CALL UPON THE NAME
OF THE LORD, TO SERVE HIM WITH ONE UNANIMOUS CONSENT *AND* ONE UNITED SHOULDER
[BEARING THE YOKE OF THE LORD].
(ZEPHANIAH 3:9)

READING: 2 SAMUEL 14:15-26

WRITERS with little experience tend to think devotional writing is easy. It's not. I would say devotional writing is one of the hardest forms of book writing because of the volume involved in producing a quality, well-written devotional book. If we think of devotions as chapters rather than as little thoughts, a devotional book has a massive number of "chapters," far more than an average book. In this book, for example, there are 91 different chapters all on different topics. While some overlap, the point of each devotion is different. Having to have the skill and creativity to handle such a book, all the while trying to tie it all together somehow can be an exhausting prospect. Devotional books are usually big projects that take a lot of writing and time. If you are lucky, you won't trip over ideas too often. More often than not, however, devotional writers go through periods where they are out of ideas and must wait until new material presents itself for the writing process to continue.

This book has been no different than any other devotional experience. It's a relatively long inspirational period, covering about four years, but that still doesn't mean sitting down and writing devotions about everything that happened in that time is practical. In hindsight, some things seem different, some seem more or less important, and some things aren't processed enough to share with others. The longer I do it, the harder it is to come up with ideas off the cuff to write and present in a devotional form. After being stuck for a few days, I started noticing that some of the topics I had remaining were inspirational bits, but they weren't following the numerical order I had in place. Some were two days ahead, some four, and one or two were relevant about ten or more days ahead of where I placed them. I started writing those devotional topics that inspired me, and as I went along, I rearranged where they were. Rearranging them gave new life to my writing, and new motivation to continue in the project, right through to the end.

Rearranging this book wasn't fun. It was necessary, but it wasn't an easy process. I had a certain concept of the way the book was going to flow, and now I had to change that entire flow. It meant I had to re-order the days and move things around. I had to change how I handled the days and how I moved through my thoughts about the work. Understandably, rearranging can get confusing. It means going back and checking to make sure things were put together properly and in a way that would make sense to the reader.

I did with my book what many of us need to do at different points in our lives. Like it or not, some things in our lives need rearranging. We like to have concepts, ideals, people and situations arranged a certain way in our lives because it gives us the ability to compartmentalize everything in a way that is most comfortable for us. The problem with comfort is, after a while, we get used to it and it is not always best. We might like it and gravitate toward it, but it isn't what we need to motivate us away from where we are and launching us into something better. The order we set might make sense to us at the time, but it can quickly become disorder if we leave it long enough. If we desire to see God's order, we must rearrange our own order, our own positioning, to bring things together in a much more sensible – and spiritual – manner.

- Day 84 -
Our Sticky Situations

> EVEN SO CONSIDER YOURSELVES ALSO DEAD TO SIN *AND* YOUR RELATION TO IT BROKEN, BUT ALIVE TO GOD [LIVING IN UNBROKEN FELLOWSHIP WITH HIM] IN CHRIST JESUS. LET NOT SIN THEREFORE RULE AS KING IN YOUR MORTAL (SHORT-LIVED, PERISHABLE) BODIES, TO MAKE YOU YIELD TO ITS CRAVINGS *AND* BE SUBJECT TO ITS LUSTS *AND* EVIL PASSIONS. DO NOT CONTINUE OFFERING OR YIELDING YOUR BODILY MEMBERS [AND FACULTIES] TO SIN AS INSTRUMENTS (TOOLS) OF WICKEDNESS. BUT OFFER *AND* YIELD YOURSELVES TO GOD AS THOUGH YOU HAVE BEEN RAISED FROM THE DEAD TO [PERPETUAL] LIFE, AND YOUR BODILY MEMBERS [AND FACULTIES] TO GOD, PRESENTING THEM AS IMPLEMENTS OF RIGHTEOUSNESS.
> (ROMANS 6:11-13)

READING: 2 SAMUEL 11:1-17

A few years ago, I found a homemade Twix bar recipe online and I wanted to try making it. I don't know why, since it's so much easier to just walk up the street to Wal-Mart or Harris Teeter and buy a bag. It sounded like a challenge at first, and I like to have stuff that's made without a lot of preservatives and additives. Thus, I set out one afternoon, while packing for a trip to Tucson and cleaning the kitchen, to make homemade Twix bars.

The recipe had three steps: the bottom shortbread layer, a caramel layer, and a top chocolate layer. Sounds easy enough, right? All was going fine until I reached the caramel, because I made two substitutions in the recipe when I got to it. In place of dark corn syrup, I did a brown sugar/water mix. and in place of sweetened condensed milk, I used evaporated milk. It wasn't coming out bad, but it wasn't coming out right, either. It was runnier than the recipe described it to be, and I kept trying to thicken it some by adding more sugar. I finally got frustrated after the third addition and turned the stove up slightly so it would boil, then I could cool it and let it cook as thick as it was going to get and then pour it over the shortbread layer and refrigerate it to cool. Having to refrigerate it meant it was going to get harder anyway, right?

I turned away for a very, very short period of time – if it was for two minutes, it was a long time. It was just long enough to clear out the sink and put a dish or two in my dishwasher. When I turned back around, I discovered caramel boiling over the pot and onto the stove top. Quick thinking, I turned it off and started to clean up what can only be described as a sticky, icky mess. The caramel had boiled over and under the burner, under the catch-all pan under the burner, and ran over top of the stove, as well. Fiona ran into the kitchen, hoping some would run off the stove so she could eat it. I just stood there, shook my head, and started to clean it up. A two-minute turnaround caused me nearly 45 minutes of cleaning up a messy situation. I was truly grateful to God that I was standing right there, and that the situation had not been made worse by walking away or not realizing the pot was boiling over.

As I was cleaning up the mess (which, believe it or not, was not my worst kitchen disaster ever!), God began to reveal to me about the often sticky and icky situations into which we get ourselves. How many of us just turn our head for that one moment, only to have a mess form in that quick, short period of time? After the sticky situation has been made, how long does it take for us to clean it up? Standing in that kitchen today, I was very aware that the second we stop paying attention is the moment we "boil over" and mess comes forth. There is a reason the Word alerts us to be aware and always prepared. Many messes we find ourselves in could be avoided if we sit up, pay attention, and stop turning to the right or left to do something else because we are bored, frustrated, or otherwise uninterested with the task at hand.

What is God calling you to focus on, right now? Where is He calling your attention? What is distracting you, or what distractions do you face? Remember, that little tiny diversion – the one you don't even think can matter – can wind up causing you a lot of trouble, clean-up, and hassle later in time.

- Day 85 -
Needful Things

AND NO MARVEL; FOR SATAN HIMSELF IS TRANSFORMED INTO AN ANGEL OF LIGHT.
THEREFORE IT IS NO GREAT THING IF HIS MINISTERS ALSO BE TRANSFORMED
AS THE MINISTERS OF RIGHTEOUSNESS; WHOSE END SHALL BE ACCORDING TO THEIR WORKS.
(2 CORINTHIANS 11;14-15, KJV)

READING: SONG OF SOLOMON 2:12-17

IN the movie *Needful Things* (based on the 1991 Stephen King novel of the same name), we see a perfect rendition of the insidious, orchestrated way the devil operates. The devil (played by Max Von Sydow), operating under the name "Leland Gaunt," moves into a small town in Maine and opens a store called "Needful Things." On the outside, it looks like any other second-hand or antique store. Upon closer inspection, we discover that the items in this store aren't just any ordinary items. Each item in that store has some sort of connection or tie to someone's childhood, such as a favorite toy that was lost, causing an emotional tie associated with that item. When someone comes into the store, the item is suggested to the customer, eliciting that emotional tie, that memory, to that item. Instead of buying and paying for those objects, they are asked to do a "favor" for the devil. Whether it's dirtying someone's clean laundry (causing an intense rift between neighbors) or some other prank, the ultimate end builds until people are committing murder against one another.

The one in the movie who was more discerning than everyone else was the sheriff, played by Ed Harris. He was the proverbial "outsider," the one who was originally from the big city and moved to the small city to try and get away from inner city craziness. His objectivity led him to discernment, to see that all these events could not have possibly been unconnected and tracked it all back to the devil himself, Leland Gaunt.

The thing many people probably miss is the devil didn't start out overt with someone, telling them to kill the other person. He started out insidiously, with one little thing and another, all in the pursuit of this one thing that elicited need in the individual. Satan didn't appear in someone's life demanding they do something so evil they would immediately retreat – he appeared, offering to meet a need, playing on people's emotions, and asking them to make little compromises here and there in pursuit of getting that need met. He made it completely justifiable, something that someone could write off, saying, "Well, this thing means a lot to me, so I'll just do this little thing. It's just a little thing!"

We are so used to dramatic movies like *The Exorcist*, *The Omen*, and *Rosemary's Baby* that we have forgotten Satan doesn't start out with us in big, dramatic ways. There isn't a soul alive who wakes up in the morning and sets themselves out to be demonically possessed that day. Nobody's head is going to spin around, nor spit out split pea soup and projectile vomit it (that's what special effects are for) when they are operating in a demonic spirit. No, Satan operates much more quietly: he offers us everything we think we need to get whatever it is we want.

If you want to see progress in your spiritual life, watch your "needful things." Listen to discernment. Idols don't become idols just because they exist; they become idols because we attach concepts to certain things, and we are willing to compromise to make those concepts become working realities for us. The devil comes roaming around along with his workers to every one of us at a certain point in time, fully aware of what to provide as he offers us everything we think we want or need...if we are willing to only do him a little "favor!"

- Day 86 -
The Fullness of Time

EVEN SO WE, WHEN WE WERE CHILDREN, WERE IN BONDAGE UNDER THE ELEMENTS
OF THE WORLD: BUT WHEN THE FULNESS OF THE TIME WAS COME, GOD SENT FORTH
HIS SON, MADE OF A WOMAN, MADE UNDER THE LAW, TO REDEEM THEM THAT WERE UNDER
THE LAW, THAT WE MIGHT RECEIVE THE ADOPTION OF SONS. AND BECAUSE YE ARE SONS,
GOD HATH SENT FORTH THE SPIRIT OF HIS SON INTO YOUR HEARTS, CRYING, ABBA, FATHER.
WHEREFORE THOU ART NO MORE A SERVANT, BUT A SON; AND IF A SON,
THEN AN HEIR OF GOD THROUGH CHRIST.
(GALATIANS 4:3-7, KJV)

READING: PSALM 104:19-28

MY book, *Awakening Christian Ministry: The Call To Serve Others As We Serve Jesus Christ* was published in 2014, but the writing process took much longer than the average book I write. The nearly seven-year process was, at times, very discouraging. The form I took in writing the book was different than all other books I have written. I've never had to write something and leave it for long periods of time and then work on it again and leave it, and then come back to it, yet again, and leave it some more. I knew there was one major revision required, and I was terribly intimidated to take it on. There were a few additional things that needed to be done, as well, to round out the book. God would have me pick up the book, work some here and there, but leave the major and final things. I never understood why, because usually I try to tackle what is most major and then handle smaller things.

About two weeks before finishing the book, God let me know it was time to finish it. I was a little intimidated at the thought. I hadn't worked on it much in the months prior, save revising some sections and waiting on what was next for it. I had one major revision still left to complete. There were still a few odds and ends, here and there, that needed tweaking, adding, or subtracting. The book itself was already over 300 pages, and it was still growing. Yet...for some reason, working on it this time was different. The revisions went quickly, and the major revision was relatively smooth, without a lot of hassle or difficulty. As I worked on it, I couldn't believe how intimidated I was by the thought of taking it on again!

I was able to handle all that was needed with my book because the fullness of its time had come. This means God does things when everything is perfect for them to be done. Even Jesus had to come at the exact opportune time: He couldn't have come into the world early, nor too late. Everything had to be set up, purposed, and prepared for Jesus to come, right at the right time. The same is true for everything we undertake. Often, we are pressing and pushing in to do things when it is not the right time to do, all because we want to see them come to pass. In a church that has picked up the world's haste-factor - believing everything should be done quickly, grandly, and loudly - we don't think about the power of timing. Timing is about more than just us being ready; it also considers the situation within the world and the various spiritual and external factors that need to be ready and receptive to receive whatever comes forth. Just like the world needed to be ready for the coming of Christ, so too the world needs to be ready (and only God can define what "ready" in each context means) for whatever God has given you to do. We love to talk about being the sons and daughters of God, but we forget that part of being His sons and daughters means we are attune and ready for His word in our lives, and waiting in obedience for the fullness of time to come for us.

The world wasn't ready for my book in 2010, when I originally thought it was done. In 2014, the fullness of its time had come. In its publication, it was ready to be received in its right and dutiful understanding of ministry.

- Day 87 -
Wide Awake

WHEN I WAS A CHILD, I TALKED LIKE A CHILD, I THOUGHT LIKE A CHILD, I REASONED LIKE A CHILD; NOW THAT I HAVE BECOME A MAN, I AM DONE WITH CHILDISH WAYS *AND* HAVE PUT THEM ASIDE.
(1 CORINTHIANS 13:11)

READING: EPHESIANS 4:12-16

HAVE you ever been bound by something and you didn't even know it? You didn't know, that is, until in that split second, when you were free? I'm not talking about going to a service and a preacher starts hammering you over the head about something you're bound by that never even happened, or someone who insists you have a problem that you don't have. We've all had those experiences, especially if you've been in church for any period of time. Too much of deliverance ministry has become a dramatic show we think we can market to the public, even if the whole mess isn't true. That's not what I'm talking about here. I'm talking about having something you didn't even know you had, nobody ever called it out, you never really had any repercussions from it other than that it was there, and it was something that every now and then you thought about, and then one day...in the blink of an eye...it was gone.

That was my situation. It wasn't some big, hidden, secret sin, or sin of any sort. It was one of those things I wondered about sometimes: what would have happened if things went a different way. It wasn't really a "regret," just a silent musing that would sometimes surface late at night and I couldn't sleep, or stuff was slow...and I would wonder...what would things be like had I made a different choice?

It wasn't something that had mused me for a few months, or two months, or a year, or two years...but something that had been a life undercurrent for a very long time. Then there was that moment when, all of a sudden...I realized it was gone. I was on a plane to Tucson, Arizona when it happened. I don't know God had healed me at that moment or that was just the moment I realized it, but I suddenly knew something was different, something that had formerly been there now was no longer. It was there, connected to this one issue, that I never received an answer to in my late-night thoughts and inner questions, but somehow, I realized the answers didn't matter anymore, and I would not need to think of them again. In a split second, I was wide awake.

The song *Wide Awake* by Katy Perry details – as does the video – a process of deliverance that happens when you have that moment in which you can let go of whatever happened and the results that followed. In the video, Katy Perry doesn't just knock out "Prince Charming," she knocks out the concept of Prince Charming – of anything that charms or enchants us, of things that seem one way, but are another, or things that draw us away from who we are and who we are meant to be. The ultimate deliverance – smashing the fantasy that held us away from where we need to be – only comes about when we stop wondering how that fantasy would have materialized. The reality is that had we done something different, entertained whatever it was, or done something else – we'd have a different reality, not the fantasy we created in our minds.

There comes a time in the life of every believer where it's time to grow up and accept the work God is doing within you. Sometimes we must walk away from things, be they people, relationships, family members, friends, and yes, even hopes, dreams, and fantasies, the little things that keep us wondering what might have happened "if," and just step up so God can take us wherever He desires us to be. Thank God for freedom.

Yeah, I'm letting go, tonight.

- Day 88 -
Selah

With my voice I cry to the Lord, and He hears and answers me out of His holy hill. Selah [pause, and calmly think of that]! I lay down and slept; I wakened again, for the Lord sustains me. I will not be afraid of ten thousands of people who have set themselves against me round about. Arise, O Lord; save me, O my God! For You have struck all my enemies on the cheek; You have broken the teeth of the ungodly. Salvation belongs to the Lord; May Your blessing be upon Your people. Selah [pause, and calmly think of that]!
(Psalm 3:4-8)

Reading: Habakkuk 3:1-13

THE word *selah* has gotten thrown around since it was popularized by a musical group who used it as their main identifying theme. What we do know of *selah* is that it is found in the Bible 74 times, 71 in Psalms and three in Habakkuk's third chapter. It is most definitely some sort of musical notation, but its exact meaning is unknown. What we do know of it, however, can be explained in the following as either one or all the following explanations: as a musical note, to indicate the musical sounds should be louder, to join two different thoughts together, to divide thoughts, or as a way to think about a command given.

Sometimes God brings us to a *selah* moment so we will look at our lives and realize we need to drop some people and things off before we can move into a new phase of our lives. He forces us to stop, pause, and look at everything and everyone differently than we have in the past. Yes, there are people who care about us, but who just don't have enough interest, motivation, or desire to do what needs to be done and to be there when you need them. It's difficult to be in seasons and situations where you don't really feel like anyone is there to care for you or to take your issues into their prayer closet because everyone is so focused on their own. It's a lot harder to live it, and to stand around and realize that if you want change to come, you must change most of the people who are around you.

To get to where we want to be, we need to stop and consider where we are and what it will take to go to the next place. Sometimes, in those interims, we need to stop looking for a word, stop relying on those who are around us, and stop and think about God. If we don't want to make the mistakes of the past, we must pause, stop jumping around with the thrill of the words "It's a new season!" reiterated every time we get in church, and learn to tell the true from the false in a deeper sense. We need to know God, we need to know times and seasons for ourselves, and I really feel we need to listen to and embrace true teachers.

When our standards increase and we expect more of those around us as well as ourselves, our seasons will shift. Only when we stop and pause to think about important things will we realize where God desires us to be. More than where we are going, we will realize what we need to gain from the season we are currently in. God doesn't shift every week, every day, every time someone gets on Facebook and wants to speak a word over us. It's not over, we aren't coming out, it's not already done, and we are not always harvesting. These things might encourage us, but they don't encourage us to do right and stand back as we have our *selah* moments. In God, we will stay right where we are until we are ready to move forward. God knows when that will be, and that means the time for our shift is in His hour...definitely not ours. We can dance, shout, scream, speak in tongues, go to a million conferences, get slain in the Spirit every time, and believe whatever we want, but to quote a famous phrase, "It ain't over 'til it's over."

Here's to change. Here's to new beginnings. Here's to the growth God wants us to have. Here's to new seasons that are new, for real, when God knows we are ready. Here's to leaving the past behind. Here's to God: yesterday, today, and forever. *Selah*.

- Day 89 -
Crossing Borders

FOR IN CHRIST JESUS YOU ARE ALL SONS OF GOD THROUGH FAITH. FOR AS MANY [OF YOU] AS WERE BAPTIZED INTO CHRIST [INTO A SPIRITUAL UNION AND COMMUNION WITH CHRIST, THE ANOINTED ONE, THE MESSIAH] HAVE PUT ON (CLOTHED YOURSELVES WITH) CHRIST. THERE IS [NOW NO DISTINCTION] NEITHER JEW NOR GREEK, THERE IS NEITHER SLAVE NOR FREE, THERE IS NOT MALE AND FEMALE; FOR YOU ARE ALL ONE IN CHRIST JESUS. AND IF YOU BELONG TO CHRIST [ARE IN HIM WHO IS ABRAHAM'S SEED], THEN YOU ARE ABRAHAM'S OFFSPRING AND [SPIRITUAL] HEIRS ACCORDING TO PROMISE.
(GALATIANS 3:26-29)

READING: EPHESIANS 2:12-22

LATELY I've been thinking about the Hillsong United song, *Oceans*. It's a very popular song. It's circulated on the internet in memes where its lyrics are placed on ocean-themed backgrounds. It's a pretty song, calming and quiet, and very popular. When it starts to play, the emotional responses build as people cry...for exactly what reason? Is it because the song is pretty? Is it because it reminds us of days gone by, of things we want to do, or is it conviction? Is it an emotional response or is it a spiritual one?

When we were first looking for a building for Sanctuary, I did some virtual tours, thanks to Google Maps, of downtown Raleigh to see where available buildings might be. In the process, I learned how the city is laid out and where the common "boundaries" are. For example, northeast Raleigh is considered the ritzy area, downtown Raleigh is considered the tourist area, and southeast Raleigh is almost universally, by reputation and association, considered to be the "low-income" area. It astonished me to learn that, as I did various internet searches, to listen to the ways in which parts of

Raleigh were classified by race and to discover that on the same street, the street may still be divided across these traditional southern lines.

Most of the ministry work I have done in Raleigh has been across the lines or borders that I am not, according to popular society, supposed to cross...and I never thought about it. When I went into ministry, I wanted to cross traditional boundaries. I just had no idea the way God would do it.

I never thought I'd see the day when half of the internet would believe they were "called to the nations." Every time I scroll down my feed, I see at least two references to people pronouncing themselves "called to the nations." They can't expound on which nations they are called to, or what they are going to do when they get to "the nations," or how they are working on communicating with people once they get to "the nations," but they insist they are called...elsewhere. These are the same people who can't walk across the street and help someone there...or walk down their street and reach out to someone in need...or drive themselves across town and visit a different church.

When we ask to be led to a place where our trust is without borders, we ask the Spirit to take us beyond what is comfortable. We are asking to cross the lines that society, our churches, our families, and our own minds have established. We are asking that our call may take us wherever God wills it to go, wherever led. Walking upon the waters is about more than just literally walking on water – it is believing that no matter where God calls you, He will take you there and carry you back.

Being "called to the nations" sounds awesome, but that call to walk on water wherever He calls starts in a different way. Nobody is impressed with how far and how aggrandized you see your call. You want to see people impressed? Cross borders wherever you are. Go across the street, go next door, go down or up the street, go across your city, go across the country, go visit someone somewhere else. Prove that you aren't afraid to cross the borders created by men. If you can't go across town, there is no way you can go cross "borders" somewhere else. After all, the "nations" are all divided by borders that you can't be afraid to cross because some man put them there.

- DAY 90 -
It Ain't Over Until the Heavenly Choir Sings

[EARNESTLY] REMEMBER THE FORMER THINGS, [WHICH I DID] OF OLD; FOR I AM GOD, AND THERE IS NO ONE ELSE; I AM GOD, AND THERE IS NONE LIKE ME, DECLARING THE END *AND* THE RESULT FROM THE BEGINNING, AND FROM ANCIENT TIMES THE THINGS THAT ARE NOT YET DONE, SAYING, MY COUNSEL SHALL STAND, AND I WILL DO ALL MY PLEASURE *AND* PURPOSE...
(ISAIAH 46:9-10)

READING: REVELATION 22:10-21

ABOUT a year and a half ago, I thought the season I was in was over. I was at a new phase of things. We were moving into a building, and we were starting the church work in Raleigh. I wasn't starting a new company, but was working on a new partnership that I hoped would provide a better income, as income was a major issue. All the words that people gave me pointed to the fact that this was a new season. I was even given word from one individual that I was walking into a "new season," it was a new time, and I should have faith and trust that the support would be there, and people would come.

I had my doubts. I was hesitant to enter a property contract when I was not sure we would be able to pay for it for the duration. I believed if I didn't have all twelve months upfront to pay for the property, I couldn't afford it. That was branded as a lack of faith by several people, and the word I was given encouraged me to move forward, despite my doubts. It was supposed to be a new time, a season to stretch my faith and watch God show up and show out in ways I could never have imagined.

Imagine my surprise when the season didn't end, and it was filled with the same issues of the existing season: attacks from people I covered and devoted time and attention to assisting. People leaving the ministry with hard feelings, when I did nothing to prompt such. Attacks from people outside of the ministry. Money wasn't an issue immediately, but about five months in, it became such a focal point, the lease became the only reason to continue at the property. I reached a point where I was out of money, tolerance, and was just plain tired.

God showed me I misjudged the season. I didn't misjudge it by myself; I had help with that. I assumed the season was over because I was starting something new, and it seemed like a new beginning. What really happened is that I was wrapping things up from the current season, making sure those who didn't need to be involved in the future stayed wherever they were, and I was able to move forward without them. I needed to know things to move forward. More than anything, I needed to see that I have been carrying people for a long time who need to be dropped somewhere. Instead of expecting them to grow, I have tried to work with them where they are, and in the process, I tolerated a lot of things I shouldn't have.

That's what happens when we misjudge seasons: we try to make things fit that just don't and foster things that don't work in the name of moving forward. In reality, we do nothing but stand still and spin, frustrating ourselves and feeling a lot of animosity and hard feelings. I believe that people were accurate in telling me God was in my actions, but I believe that they misjudged the results, and in the process, gave me information that was misleading.

I've become real in my own acceptance process throughout this book to help you realize it ain't over as easily as you might think it is. Just because other people tell us a season is up, it seems like we are doing something new, or we're just ready, doesn't mean the season is over. It's easy to misjudge a departing season, especially when we have help.

No matter how hard your season is, remember it's not over until the heavenly choir sings, and God makes it clear that it's over.

- Day 91 -
Divine Contradictions

We are assured *and* know that [God being a partner in their labor] all things work together *and* are [fitting into a plan] for good to *and* for those who love God and are called according to [His] design *and* purpose. For those whom He foreknew [of whom He was aware and loved beforehand], He also destined from the beginning [foreordaining them] to be molded into the image of His Son [and share inwardly His likeness], that He might become the firstborn among many brethren. And those whom He thus foreordained, He also called; and those whom He called, He also justified (acquitted, made righteous, putting them into right standing with Himself). And those whom He justified, He also glorified [raising them to a heavenly dignity and condition or state of being].
(Romans 8:28-30)

Reading: Genesis 22:1-14

SOME people say the Bible is contradictory. They believe different parts of the Bible contradict other parts. In a literal sense, they are correct. If you read the Bible like it's any other book, any other record, it doesn't make much sense. Parts say one thing, then something else, then something else, and if you try to take it all at once, it seems like a big contradiction. Looking at the Bible in this form has caused many people to abandon their faith, because they didn't take the time to learn the Bible within its own context, one situation and circumstance at a time.

I don't believe the Bible contradicts itself, because I don't seek to take the Bible in such a literal sense. I'm against the notion that we must force the Bible into our own literal printed understanding of what it means or doesn't mean. The Bible itself was written over thousands of years, and before it was written, it was spoken from one generation to another, and before that, it was experienced, live and in person. It's impossible to literally do all the things outlined from Genesis to Revelation, especially if you try to take them all at once. I believe the Bible presents many different circumstances, and its different approaches prove that different circumstances require different obedience and different answers to problems. When we look at the Bible in this light, it's not a divine contradiction; it is God, standing ever-present, acknowledging His position outside of time to try and touch the lives of those who seek Him. It proves God is with us always, even though cultures, circumstances, and yes, ideals often change.

Sometimes our walk with God feels like a contradiction if we take it too literally. We like the idea of divine chronology to feel like it makes literal sense and is easy to follow along as we go along. Our little clichés, expressions, and sayings bring us comfort because they conform to our idea of time and literal progress that we seek in the spiritual realm. The problem enters because God doesn't operate within our sense of literalism and our desire to see things happen in the strict, unbending way we tend to desire. God doesn't have to turn us inside out; instead, He just sends enough contradictions our way to shake up our literal world and turn it into a transformative experience that brings the truth of change in an undeniable way.

Some things in this book probably don't seem like they make a lot of sense if we take them more than one day at a time. They don't seem logical if we line them all up, one after the other. They might even seem contradictory. Herein lies the beauty of spiritual lessons; they are contradictory at times. They respond to each situation and circumstance we are in, and therein lies God, at the heart of everything, good and bad, working His purposes. Life isn't lived all lined up in a neat row; it's lived one day at a time, one step at a time, one moment at a time.

Things don't seem so off if we are willing to step back

and examine ourselves and what we seek in each season. In the growing process, it doesn't all make sense. On the other side of the season, it doesn't always make sense. Our experience with God is something to be lived. If we take too much of it at once, it doesn't make sense. If we are willing to take it one day at a time, one experience at a time, and one moment at a time, we will find God in anything, no matter how hard it might be to understand.

- AFTERWORD -
The End of a Season

AND SO IT WAS THAT HE [ABRAHAM], HAVING WAITED LONG *AND* ENDURED PATIENTLY, REALIZED *AND* OBTAINED [IN THE BIRTH OF ISAAC AS A PLEDGE OF WHAT WAS TO COME] WHAT GOD HAD PROMISED HIM. MEN INDEED SWEAR BY A GREATER [THAN THEMSELVES], AND WITH THEM IN ALL DISPUTES THE OATH TAKEN FOR CONFIRMATION IS FINAL [ENDING STRIFE]. ACCORDINGLY GOD ALSO, IN HIS DESIRE TO SHOW MORE CONVINCINGLY *AND* BEYOND DOUBT TO THOSE WHO WERE TO INHERIT THE PROMISE THE UNCHANGEABLENESS OF HIS PURPOSE *AND* PLAN, INTERVENED (MEDIATED) WITH AN OATH. THIS WAS SO THAT, BY TWO UNCHANGEABLE THINGS [HIS PROMISE AND HIS OATH] IN WHICH IT IS IMPOSSIBLE FOR GOD EVER TO PROVE FALSE *OR* DECEIVE US, WE WHO HAVE FLED [TO HIM] FOR REFUGE MIGHT HAVE MIGHTY INDWELLING STRENGTH *AND* STRONG ENCOURAGEMENT TO GRASP *AND* HOLD FAST THE HOPE APPOINTED FOR US *AND* SET BEFORE [US].
(HEBREWS 6:15-18)

THE quotation I placed at the beginning of this book, "Sometimes the things we cannot change end up changing us" signifies much of what I went through during these past few years. Change is never easy; going through change is even harder. I am reminded of something I told a former spiritual daughter of mine, "Transitions are hard. You aren't where you are going, and you aren't where you were. You are somewhere in the middle and being there is one of the hardest places to be." I said it, not realizing what fell out of my mouth. I was talking to her, but I was also talking to me. I wasn't into full transition at the point when I said it, but within a couple of months, I would be. Being not where you want to be but not where you were means you are somewhere else, somewhere between the two, becoming something altogether different than that which we might have easily understood at one point in time. Sure, we like to sing and muse on the concept of changing seasons and entering new things, but we often do so with careless thought and word about what change can really be like for someone else who is going through it. In every change yes, there is hope for something else, but there is also a serious sense of the end of something, the end of a current season.

I thought the hardest thing for me in the change from the season I was in, into the next one, was the total difference of my ministry. I went in one way and came out another. Its end came about in a way I did not expect, nor anticipate; it ended when I was willing to walk away from something destructive, openly admitting if it totally changed my whole life and ministry, having that effect, I was willing to take that risk. In reality, it was not the difference of my ministry that changed me; it is the literal ending of it as it existed, and as I knew it. Once I was ready to change that, in full, I was ready to change. I had invested for years in it the way it was, reaching out to specific groups of people and branding my work in ways that would be available and appealing to those people. It sounds simple enough, and like I used a sense of wisdom. I had everything constructed for them. One by one, all those things were deconstructed. By the time I had full awareness of that change and those differences, I realized the hardest thing for me to change in that season was me. I wasn't necessarily who I always thought I was, or doing what God necessarily always wanted me to do. I had grown comfortable filling a role, trying to manufacture a certain surface appearance and style that would work for the audience I was trying to reach. Coming to the end of that – facing that fact, accepting that fact, and embracing it – was, by far, the most difficult thing I had to do. Through ups and downs, kicking and screaming, protests, rehashing, and trying to change and do things in my own way, God used my own ministry – and those I frequently ministered to – to bring about that change and revelation in me.

We talk often about the power of ministry or our

personal obedience to God to change others, but we don't ever think about the idea that God may desire to use our own ministry callings to change us, ourselves. Sometimes God puts us in difficult and seemingly impossible situations, with impossible people who refuse to change and refuse to receive what we have, because He wants to get our attention about something within us. If we are in Him and He in us, then no matter what the situation or circumstance may be, we should always embrace the idea that the "change" He seeks to work is never just within those we work with, reach out to, teach, train, lead, or associate with; He is also working something out within all of us.

It is for this reason I believe we avoid the seasonal changes. We avoid change because we hate transition, and we hate the experience of how misplaced it makes us all feel. We like feeling safe and comfortable, in the hopes that our spiritual positioning, as a metaphorical tree or plant, will continue to bloom year after year, as if we are going to just stand here by osmosis and become all we can be, without any movement from the Master's hand, whatsoever. The problem with this is it's not how natural agriculture works, and it is certainly not how spiritual agriculture works, either. Sometimes God must prune us, tend to us, uproot us and plant us somewhere else, cut us back, graft us with another plant, or somehow change our situation and circumstance. All plants go through four seasons of winter, spring, summer, and fall, and as we move through our seasons, we change, we transform, and we become something else as the situations and experiences of each change us.

As of the conclusion of this book, I am gathering my seeds, taking them into my new season, and preparing for all that is next, even if I don't understand it all. I have accepted God's transformation on my life, and I pray that you will receive His in yours, as well.

My specific prayer for you today is that you will not fear change, because I can stand here today and tell you, it is worth every trial and difficulty to achieve. It is as simple as receiving the truth that sometimes the things we cannot change end up changing us, because that is their exact purpose. Don't quit. Don't give up; just change. Let the change that needs to come forth in you come forth. Listen to God speaking through the circumstances that might not be exactly what you hoped or dreamed for and let Him show you what you need to do. Don't think you are nothing, or will be nothing, or that you are on or off track all of the time. You might not understand the route by which God is carrying you to your destiny but know that if you are yielding to the Spirit, you will get where you are totally supposed to be. It might be far from where you start, but it doesn't mean what you've done or where you've been is of no value. It was part of a journey, it was part of an era that had a purpose, destiny, and an insight, all its own, for that season. As one era, and one season, pass from one space to another, take your seeds. Take those things, visions, lessons, and insights God has given to you from where you've been and plant them, because they all are there for that very purpose. We don't leave things behind in the sense of abandoning them; we take them with us, in the form of learning and growing, and with those seeds, become something beyond that which you could never imagine as you bloom where you are planted in your new season to come.

- About the Author -

Dr. Lee Ann B. Marino, Ph.D., D.Min., D.D. (she/her) is "everyone's favorite theologian" leading Gen X, Millennials, and Gen Z with expertise in leadership training, queer and feminist theology, general religion, and apostolic theology. She has served in ministry since 1998 and was ordained as a pastor in 2002 and an apostle in 2010. She founded what is now Sanctuary Apostolic Fellowship Empowerment (SAFE) Ministries in 2004. Under her ministry heading Dr. Marino is founder and Overseer of Sanctuary International Fellowship Tabernacle (SIFT) (the original home of National Coming Out Sunday) and The Sanctuary Network, and Chancellor of Apostolic Covenant Theological Seminary (ACTS).

Affectionately nicknamed "the Spitfire," Dr. Marino has spent over two decades as an "apostle, preacher, and teacher" (2 Timothy 1:11), exercising her personal mandate to become "all things to all people" (1 Corinthians 9:22). Her embrace of spiritual issues (both technical and intimate) has found its home among both seekers and believers, those who desire spiritual answers to today's issues.

Dr. Marino has preached throughout the United States, Puerto Rico, and Europe in hundreds of religious services and experiences throughout the years. A history maker in her own right, she has spent over two decades in advocacy, education, and work for and within minority spiritual communities (including African American, Hispanic, and LGBTQ+). She has also served as the first woman on all-male synods, councils, and panels, as well as the first preacher or speaker welcomed of a different race, sexual orientation, or identity among diverse communities. Today, Dr. Marino's work extends to over 150 countries as she hosts the popular *Kingdom Now* podcast, which is in the top 20 percentile of all podcasts worldwide. She is also the author of over 35 books and the popular Patheos column, *Leadership on Fire*. To date, she has had five bestselling titles within their subject matter: *Understanding Demonology, Spiritual Warfare, Healing, and Deliverance: A Manual for the Christian Minister*; *Ministry School Boot Camp: Training for Helps Ministries, Appointments, and Beyond*; *Discovering Intimacy: A Journey Through the Song of Solomon*; *Fruit of the Vine: Study and Commentary on the Fruit of the Spirit*; and *Ministering to LGBTQ+ (and Those Who Love Them): A Primer for Queer Theology* (and its accompanying workbook).

As a public icon and social media influencer, Dr. Marino advocates healthy body image (curvy/full-figured), representation as a demisexual/aromantic, and albinism awareness as a model. Known to those she works with, she is a spiritual mom, teacher, leader, professor, confidant, and friend. She continues to transform, receiving new teaching, revelation, and insight in this thing we call "ministry." Through years of spiritual growth and maturity, Dr. Marino stands as herself, here to present what God has given to her for any who have an ear to hear.

For more information, visit her website at kingdompowernow.org.

www.ingramcontent.com/pod-product-compliance
Lightning Source LLC
Chambersburg PA
CBHW032058090426
42743CB00007B/163